Customer Service at a Crossroads

"What You Do Next to Improve Performance Will Determine Your Company's Destiny"

Matt McConnell

Dr. Jon Anton

Business Navigation

Only two centuries ago, early explorers (adventurous business executives of those bygone days) were guided primarily with a compass and celestial navigation using reference points like the North Star. Today's busy executive also needs guidance systems with just-in-time business intelligence to navigate through the challenges of locating, recruiting, keeping, and growing profitable customers. The Anton Press provides this navigational system through practical, how-to-do-it books for the modern day business executive.

2nd Edition Copyright © 2003 (6-Jun-03)

The Anton Press, Santa Maria, CA 93455
Used pursuant to license. All rights reserved.

No part of this publication may be copied, scanned or reproduced without the written permission of the Anton Press, a division of BenchmarkPortal, Inc.,
3130 Skyway Drive, Suite 702,
Santa Maria, CA 93455.

ISBN 0-9719652-6-9

Dedication

This book is dedicated to all of those that believed in and encouraged this vision. It is the culmination of nearly a decade of work that was sustained and developed by the brightest minds in business. It is my great pleasure to have worked with all of you. In particular, I would like to acknowledge, my partner in crime Tanya, my family, my business partner and friend John McIlwaine, Ed and Bonnie Evans, Rusty Gordon, Tracy McAllister, Caran Snitz, Jon Anton and the entire team at Knowlagent and BenchmarkPortal that made this book possible.

Matt McConnell

I dedicate this book to all the members of our Benchmarking Community that support our research and who respond to our One-Minute-Surveys that result in some of the more important findings presented in this book.

Dr. Jon Anton

Table of Contents

List of Figures

ACKNOWLEDGEMENTS

We would wish to thank our analytic team, including Deirdre Cooper, Ric Latendresse and Dave Machin, for their attention to statistical detail and database mining.

We also wish to thank our production team, including Debi Cloud, Susan Hampton, and Gail Carver, for their very professional work in taking our numerous drafts of the manuscript, and transforming its many words, graphs, and tables into an attractive and readable book.

by

J.D. Power III
Chairman and CEO

One contact at a time.

That's how customer relationships are won and sustained. Unfortunately, it's also how they are lost. While there have been many books written about customer satisfaction and how to build lifetime customer loyalty, we find ourselves in some very different— and difficult times.

Several of the concepts surrounding customer service that precede this book remain valid, yet a paradigm shift with regard to the value of a company's customer service center requires new strategies and unique approaches. Creating a competitive differentiator based on products and services is increasingly difficult, if not impossible. As a result, the key distinction organizations typically can make is in the quality of the customer's experience. The customer service center, historically considered as expensive overhead and a cost to be controlled, is now a significant, strategic player in an organization's ability to retain and maintain critical customer relationships and drive revenues.

As executives continue to realize the importance of customer service centers, traditional metrics such as average handle time, hold time and first call resolution will turn toward metrics that deliver more value to the organization: the effectiveness of customer interactions. At that point, organizations will hold customer service agents responsible for meeting the needs of each individual customer instead of how quickly they can get the customer off the phone. For customer service agents to perform under these measures, however, they will need the knowledge and skills required to deliver the results in this new environment, where customer is king.

As customer service centers re-evaluate the balance between efficiency and customer care, the scales are tipping toward the objectives and goals of their organization's customer relationship management (CRM) initiatives. While companies committed to CRM have already invested significant financial and human capital to deliver a single view of their customers to agents, there is a disconnect in agents' skills and ability to effectively use the technology and the information to transform a customer contact into a valued relationship.

One of the lessons learned with CRM over the past few years is that CRM is more than software. Successful CRM implementations require services, business plans and a tight working relationship between customer and vendor. Many companies considered CRM software as a silver bullet that can solve their customer relationship problems. But if the "R" in the acronym CRM truly stands for "relationship," technology alone can hardly transform a company into a customer-centric organization. The research that I have been involved in related to what makes or breaks CRM initiatives shows that focusing on improving customer relationships by altering how business is conducted and changing employee performance often mark the difference between CRM success and failure.

When companies realize that the value of their CRM investment can only be realized if agents are properly measured and trained to leverage those technologies, the customer service center could become the centerpiece of many organization's CRM strategies.

By consistently delivering information about products, services and information to customer service agents, based on their individual skill gaps and knowledge deficiencies — at the right time in the right way, organizations are also delivering a consistent, clear understanding of corporate objectives and vision. The result: thousands of customer interactions that delight the customer and improve retention. And in many cases, this in turn can result in improved profitability.

Organizations that fail to make the connection between the performance of their agents and the realization of their vision of customer service and retention strategies will be doomed to failure. The customer service center agent represents an untapped resource and potential within an organization. Optimizing agent performance can quickly deliver incredible returns beyond customer loyalty.

That is what this book is all about.

Survival for today's major corporations depends on the ability to maintain revenue growth and a satisfied customer base. Most large companies generate the majority of their revenue (80%) from existing customers. While the numbers vary, experts agree that it costs more to attract a new customer than to keep an existing one.

After years of consolidation and growth through mergers and acquisitions, large companies, in mature industries, are unable to maintain growth. In addition, entering untapped markets for new meaningful growth is high risk and has become increasingly difficult. As a result, existing customers are not only the most significant and profitable revenue source, but they represent the best opportunity for future growth and continued success and survival. This is one of the most fundamental principles of business. So what's the big deal, you ask?

Here it is. Ironically, the most neglected organization in the company has been charged with managing its most valuable asset— its customers. The heritage of customer service and the customer service center makes it the least likely nominee to lead business strategy. The organization has never been considered strategic in the past and it has suffered through years of commensurate under investment. That is all about to change.

In response to a major competitive threat from Japanese manufacturing, W. Edwards Deming authored a book called *Out of The Crisis*. The book was written as a call to action for American companies to adopt a radical new model for manufacturing or risk becoming extinct. The work of Deming and others became the catalyst for a major transformation in business and is the foundation of all modern manufacturing processes.

Today, on the shop floor of the information economy—the customer service center, there is an alarming similarity to old-line manufacturing. The organizational, functional and management parallels between the group that manages the customer today and the group that manufactured products forty years ago, are remarkable. In particular, the manufacturing crisis of the late—

1970's and the customer service crossroads of today bear a resemblance worth noting.

In a study conducted by the Harvard Business Review (The Growth Crisis, July 2002), once financial engineering and international expansion are stripped away, there has been little or no core growth in the largest companies in America in the last decade. In order to survive and remain viable, companies must re-think the way in which they serve their customers. There are lessons that can be learned from the crisis in manufacturing and there are unique challenges that can be overcome in a unique way.

After years of researching the customer service center, we have developed several principles for building best performers. We have distilled our findings into the basic laws that govern success and failure in the market and provide them here for you to adopt.

The Growth/Profit Requirement

Companies are in the "business" of making a profit. Without it, there isn't a tomorrow. In order for there to be a tomorrow, growth in revenue and profits is absolutely required. According to a new study by Accenture, *How Much Are Customer Relationships Really Worth?*, today the most profitable companies are those that make the smartest decisions about allocating resources to marketing, sales and service (Dull, Stephens and Wolfe, 2002). This study reveals which business improvements are the most effective in attracting and retaining customers. The study shows a strong link between a company's overall excellence in dealing with customers, or their "Customer Capabilities," and their financial performance (figure 1.1).

According to the Accenture study, a typical $1 billion business unit could add $40 million in profit by enhancing their customer-facing capabilities by 10%. The second set of findings show that the top business improvement initiatives that produce the highest impact on financial performance are

- customer service,
- converting customer information into business intelligence,
- motivating and rewarding employees,
- attracting and retaining employees, and
- developing sales and service skills in employees.

Notice that employees appear in three out of five of the above impact areas, reinforcing the most fundamental and important business principle in the world: business is done between people. If that same business, in our example, ramped up its performance by 30 percent, thereby propelling itself from say *average* to *high* Customer Capabilities, it could improve its pretax profit by as much as $120 million.

Cause and Effect

Accenture research has identified 21 customer capabilities that, when a company improves them, can have a significant impact on return on sales. For example, return on sales at a typical U.S.$1billion company can rise by as much as U.S.$13 million if the company improves its performance by 30 percent - that is, from average to high performance - in either customer service or by motivating/rewarding employees.

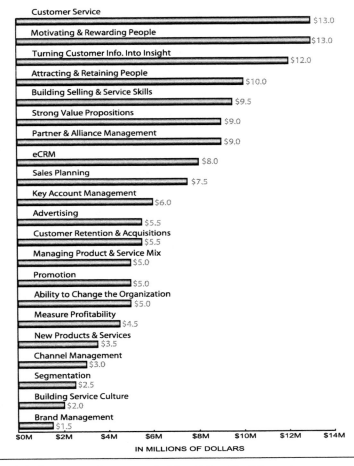

Capability	Value
Customer Service	$13.0
Motivating & Rewarding People	$13.0
Turning Customer Info. Into Insight	$12.0
Attracting & Retaining People	$10.0
Building Selling & Service Skills	$9.5
Strong Value Propositions	$9.0
Partner & Alliance Management	$9.0
eCRM	$8.0
Sales Planning	$7.5
Key Account Management	$6.0
Advertising	$5.5
Customer Retention & Acquisitions	$5.5
Managing Product & Service Mix	$5.0
Promotion	$5.0
Ability to Change the Organization	$5.0
Measure Profitability	$4.5
New Products & Services	$3.5
Channel Management	$3.0
Segmentation	$2.5
Building Service Culture	$2.0
Brand Management	$1.5

$0M $2M $4M $6M $8M $10M $12M $14M

IN MILLIONS OF DOLLARS

Figure 1.1. Accenture's research identifies the 21 customer capabilities that, when improved, have a significant impact on return on sales.

4

The Accenture research is further validated by a simple, yet powerful observation made by University of Michigan Business School Professor Claes Fornell (Siebel, 2002). He said, "As long as customers have a choice to go somewhere else, and as long as repeat business is important, companies must deliver the highest levels of customer satisfaction in order to stay in business."

> The Internet puts the customer in charge. It's easy for customers to find today's best bargains, information once jealously guarded up and down the supply chain. For many companies, customer's ignorance was a profit center.
> —Gary Hamel, in *BusinessWeek*, "The Search for the Young and Gifted" Oct 4, 1999.

Let's examine in more depth the drivers relating to customer satisfaction and retention. When a customer's loyalty (an indicator of retention) increases, a beneficial "flywheel" (figure 1.2) kicks in (Siebel, 2002), powered by

- increase purchases of existing products,
- cross-purchases of a company's other products,
- price premium due to appreciation of your added-value services,
- reduced operating costs because of a customer's familiarity with the service system of your company, and
- positive word of mouth in terms of referring other customers to your company.

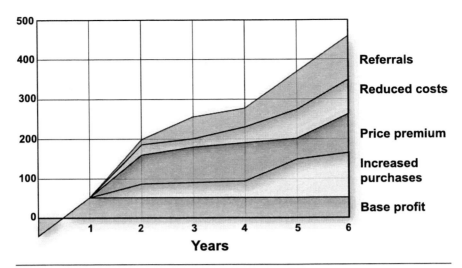

Figure 1.2. The value of one customer

So who is responsible for making sure this powerful flywheel gains momentum? The Board of Directors sets this wheel in motion by providing customer satisfaction objectives, which ultimately drive revenue and profits since profit growth is what drives the financial markets over the long term. The Board of Directors purpose is to essentially generate and protect shareholder value. So if customer satisfaction is the objective, who is responsible for executing this strategy? The executives in a company are the ones who must implement these objectives.

Let's look at a real life example and the objectives AT&T executives choose to focus on. In this six-year study AT&T (T. Lian, 1994), compared their *market share* to *customer perceived value*. The results are shown in figure 1.3. This figure shows a period of time during which AT&T was reengineered completely to make customers number one. Notice how the market share parallels the customer-perceived value exactly.

Research has shown that customer perceived value and satisfaction are excellent leading predictors of next year's revenue, market share and profits. Executives have learned that long-term profit growth requires long-term revenue growth. This is because expense reduction is a short-term solution to profit growth. Companies can only reduce expenses for so long before revenues begin to decline as a result of fewer and fewer resources. So what decisions and strategies should corporate executives be focused on today? If we learn from the AT&T and Accenture examples, we can see that the focus should be on improving their customer-perceived value or their customer capabilities.

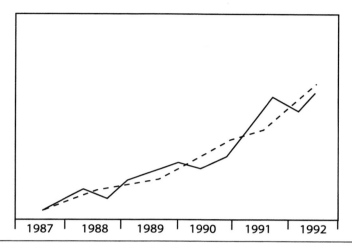

Figure 1.3. Customer perceived value and market share at AT&T

According to Roland T. Rust, Director of the Center for e-Service at the University of Maryland and coauthor of the book *Driving Customer Equity*, information technology is the key catalyst in the rise of the service economy. "The shift toward a service economy and the rise of the information economy are two sides of the same coin. Technology allows companies to take advantage of the service economy's emphasis on the customer's experience."

Rust also notes that relationship-based companies are also inherently focused more on building revenue than on cutting costs. This is another critical factor in business success. "Companies adopting a revenue perspective earn better profits, both in terms of return on assets and stock appreciation, than companies that emphasize cost reductions or try to emphasize cost-cutting and revenue-building at the same time. That is because there is a limit to how much organizations can reduce costs before they start hurting the business, but there isn't any real upper limit on revenues."

According to Professor Fornell (Siebel, 2002), "For a large capitalization company, a five percent increase in customer satisfaction is related to an average $3.25 billion increase in market capitalization." This also means that a 1% increase in customer satisfaction relates to a 3% increase in market cap. Since it is more cost effective to sell to an existing customer than to acquire a new one, customer satisfaction has gone from a "nice to have" to a "must have."

Fornell has developed the American Customer Satisfaction Index (ACSI). It is a national economic indicator for the U.S. He has also developed indices for Europe, Korea, South America and Malaysia. The ACSI indicates customer satisfaction with the quality of goods and services available to consumers. The index shows that market value added (MVA), stock price and return on investment are highly related to ACSI.

Why is there a relationship between customer satisfaction and shareholder value? The reason lies in the relationship between the investors' valuation of a company and the sources of a company's cash flow, i.e., its customers. Market capitalization, says Fornell, "is the same as the net present value of the expected cash flows. With few exceptions, these cash flows accrue from two sources: current customers and new customers. Since the flow of cash is higher from current customers, the satisfaction of a company's current customers has a large impact on shareholder value." In addition, his research shows that organizations that maintain a steady state of improvement in customer satisfaction over a period of years gain an increasing rate of improvement in their profitability. A company that improves its customer satisfaction scores by 1% a year over 5 successive years will on average accumulate an increase of 11.5% return on investment over the same time period.

The Strategic Real Estate: The Customer Service Center

So it seems that the key strategy to profit growth would then be to focus on customers; especially existing ones. Figure 1.4 shows the value of a satisfied customer (Anton, 2002).

While this strategy seems more than obvious, why are companies struggling to make a profit or to grow? To sustain real, core growth companies must either sell more products and services to existing customers or acquire more customers, faster. Revenue growth, and, therefore, profit growth seems to be harder and harder to generate the larger a company becomes. In fact, according to the Harvard Business Review, from 1990 to 2000, just 10% of publicly traded companies enjoyed eight or more years of double-digit growth in their top line (Slywotzky, 2002). Once the growth is stripped away from acquisitions and price increases, many of the world's largest companies showed very little core growth over the last decade.

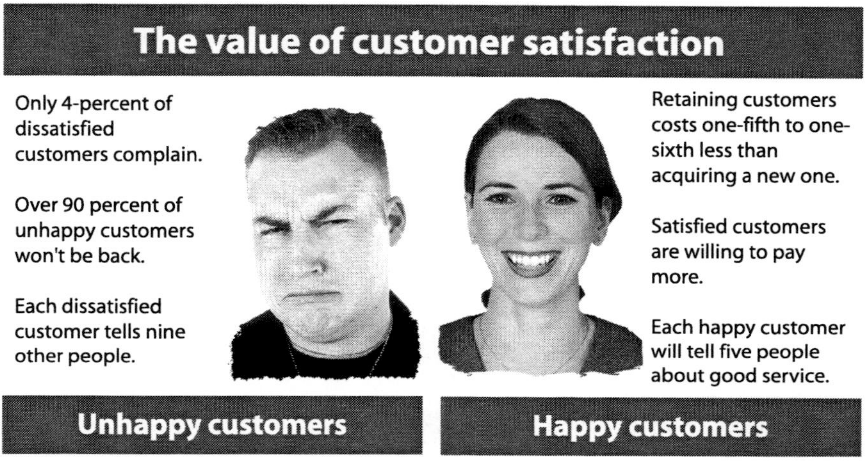

The value of customer satisfaction

Only 4-percent of dissatisfied customers complain.

Over 90 percent of unhappy customers won't be back.

Each dissatisfied customer tells nine other people.

Retaining customers costs one-fifth to one-sixth less than acquiring a new one.

Satisfied customers are willing to pay more.

Each happy customer will tell five people about good service.

Unhappy customers

Happy customers

Figure 1.4. The value of a satisfied customer

Customer satisfaction is at the heart of achieving the competitive advantage, according to Rust. "Over the past fifty years our economy has shifted from an industrial economy to a service economy. This economic transformation also shifts the emphasis from transactions to relationships. The companies that can establish superior customer relationships are the ones that will win."

So how does a company create and manage superior customer experiences? According to a recent study by Gartner, while companies may be trying to save money by driving customers to use self-service, 92% of all customers get in touch with businesses through the customer service center (figure 1.5) (Knowlagent, 2002). Also, as many as 70% of all business transactions occur over the telephone. So the question is, what is standing between the executive and their customer? Of course, for most companies, it is the customer service center. In spite of the emergence of new channels and Web applications for customer self-service, the bottom line is that people have relationships, not computers, hence customer service agents own the customer experience.

In an era where products and services are increasingly becoming commodities, customer satisfaction in each and every interaction with an organization is a key success factor. The importance of customer service can be gauged by the fact that two-thirds of customers stop doing business with a particular organization because of service-related problems. For example, a survey of bank customers in the United States found "ease of doing business" as the principal factor and "quality of service" as the second most important factor in choosing a financial institution.

Customer Service Center Agents <u>OWN</u> the Customer Relationship-

From the Gartner Group

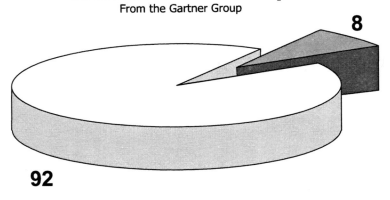

8

92

☐ **Customers Using Customer Service Centers**

▨ **Customers Using Self-Service**

Figure 1.5. 92% of all customers still get in touch with businesses through customer service centers (source, Gartner).

Because the lion's share of contact between an organization and their customers goes through a customer service agent, these employees, in essence, form a layer between the executives of an organization and the customer. What makes that layer so dense and complex? If it were simple, it would be easily implemented and operated. The barrier is made up of a range of things that includes the sale, delivery and use of the product or service. In an ideal world the sale and delivery of the product would be easy and on time. The use of the product would be clear. Companies would produce products that came with clear, explicit instructions on their use, they would always meet our expectations and they would not break. The billing statements would be clear, intuitive and always correct. Marketing programs would be targeted so that consumers would be compelled to buy without the urging of a salesperson to close the deal. In that world, customer service centers would not be necessary.

However, we clearly do not live in that world. In our world, instructions are challenging, products are over marketed, consumer expectations can be unrealistic and products do break—a lot. Billing statements are supposed to be designed to meet the needs of everyone to ensure prompt payment, yet often fail to meet the needs of anyone. Take for instance your phone bill. Almost everyone has had some charge on a bill that they do not understand. This requires that the customer take time out to call the customer service center and the company must take time (which is money) to answer that non-revenue generating call. And marketing to consumers might be easier if they were not so fickle, finicky, and therefore, downright difficult to model. What is "hot" today, is not "hot" tomorrow. What is perceived as value (something they would open up their wallet for) by consumers changes daily. Because of the world we live in, companies need customer service centers.

In many ways some executives can't handle the truth about their company's dependence on the customer service center. Service centers for many executives still hold that place of "necessary but not essential" to doing business. In fact, most executives come from the days when a customer service center was the lowest common denominator in a business—that sweatshop in the basement that talks to customers when they complain. Who would have thought that the customer service center agents would become the ambassadors of the company? They hold the keys to the kingdom. The performance of each customer service center agent—how well he or she can convert thousands of customer contacts into revenue-producing sales and/or solid relationships that produce the all-elusive feelings of customer loyalty—therefore, substantially impacts an organization's bottom line. It logically follows, then, that improving agent performance and aligning the mission of the customer service center with corporate objectives will allow executives to more effectively meet their strategic and financial goals.

Unfortunately, dealing with the customer service center is like going to the dentist for both the executive and the customer—an endurable pain that is almost always unpleasant. The customer service center has been the consumer's dentist office for 30 years so the executives have largely ignored it and the consumers have largely endured it. Neither has demanded its improvement—until recently.

11

This paradigm shift in thought leadership must happen for those that want to stay in business. The customer service center is the lifeline to customers and therefore to profit growth. The bottom line comes down to simply this: If you want your job (and your stock options to have some value, to be able to retire to that nice country home on the lake…), an executive must deal with the customer service center as a strategic, leveragable asset.

Some companies, in search of customer satisfaction and increased profits, have begun to view the customer service center as a strategic real estate between them and the customer's money. Competition and the ease of switching to a competitor combined with the rhetoric of world-class customer service and the occasional glimpse of it (pleasant customer service experience) has created an increasingly intolerant consumer. Some executives have reacted to the intolerant consumer by trying to hone in on what is going wrong.

We suggest a more proactive stance. Rather than be held hostage to the customer service center, dive in headfirst and begin to understand its fundamental mission. Once that is understood, you can then begin to fix it. It is not something that is going to go away, in fact, it is going to get more and more important so it has to be dealt with. Executives have to fix it because it occupies the strategic real estate between themselves and profit growth. There is no other choice but to get it right. The customer service center is a leverage-able asset of the corporation because it occupies strategic real estate in both the supplier-customer relationship and the revenue and cost generation processes.

The Fundamental Mission of the Customer Service Center

When you take a step back from the customer service center, you can see we have over-complicated a simple process. It goes something like this: a customer, with a need, contacts a company and expects someone friendly and knowledgeable to fulfill the need. They want to get their needs fulfilled and they are willing to part with their money to do so. They do not want to wait. They do not want to be transferred to someone's supervisor. They want service, and they want it NOW.

The customer expects the company to employ people that are experts on its products or services. They do not consider whether or not the company can afford to employ, train and deploy knowledgeable people to fulfill this need. They assume that the cost of doing that is built in to the product—or it darn well should be. What kind of a businessperson would sell a product that they cannot afford to support?

Have We Failed To Deliver On the Mission?

No one has to look further than personal experience to say that companies, very often, do not deliver on the fundamental mission of the customer service center. What has confounded the fundamental mission of the customer service center? We think it is a long-standing view of the customer service center as tactical as a result of an often-reinforced lack of performance.

As American consumers, an abundance of companies provide us with an almost infinite variety of products and services. As a result of the level of competition for our business, we enjoy and even demand the best. There is an anomaly in the American free market that we like to call "acceptable indifference." Americans have come to accept the indifference of certain situations that they would otherwise reject as consumers. As a result, the companies that provide those products and services build that acceptable indifference into their business models.

Take, for example, the airline industry and the wireless phone industry. How many times have you started a conversation with, "Sorry, my flight was delayed," or "I must have hit a bad cell"? We have come to accept late flights and spotty cell coverage. As a result, the executives of the airline industry have never considered 100% on time departure and arrival when they build their financial models. Executives in the wireless phone industry have never considered total coverage when they lay out their plans.

Fortunately for them, neither have their customers. Sure, there are disclaimers on the inside of the ticket jacket for all airlines. There are also disclaimers in all wireless plans and agreements. As consumers, we generally accept the delays and poor coverage. Can you imagine if that happened in healthcare (asthma medicine that worked in 60 seconds... or 2 hours)? Can you imagine if that happened in consumer products (inconsistent formulation of products)? Can you imagine how outraged you would be if your brand new car regularly died as you drove it? This acceptable indifference applies to the customer service center as well. Unfortunately, there seems to be a broad acceptance of poor performance in the customer service center. Consumers accept it and executives have built it into the business model...but does it make sense to keep going down this path or is it time to take the road less traveled?

13

What's the Problem?

The fundamental mission of the customer service center is to fulfill customer needs. Executives have thrown technology at it. Faster is not better. Executives have thrown process/measurement at it. Smarter is not better. Better is better. Service IS the differentiator.

So what is the problem? Over the years, organizations have invested billions in technology, data and process improvements, but ironically, after all that investment, only efficiencies improve, not performance. The way to a customer's heart lies not in software, systems and processes, but in people.

While organizations have made considerable expenditures to deliver calls smarter and faster to customer service agents, and to retroactively monitor employee performance with quality monitoring systems, only a fraction of investment is made to proactively ensure that your best performers are prepared to effectively handle customer calls. As a result, many organizations are simply delivering bad service to their customers faster, and investing inordinate amounts of expensive time coaching their worst customer service agents after the damage is already done to the customer relationship.

It will become even more difficult to differentiate products and services, leaving customers to increasingly rely on customer service agents for information and using it as the basis for establishing and retaining a business relationship. As a result, customer service centers have become a critical asset for businesses, being viewed as a revenue generator and more strategic rather than tactical to deepen customer relationships and increase lifetime value. Where companies put their investments moving forward—in additional systems or in people—will ultimately determine their destiny.

14

CHAPTER 2: MANAGEMENT'S ROLE IN MAKING SURE CUSTOMERS ARE DELIGHTED

The Emergence of the Modern Customer Service Center

In the first chapter it became quite clear that without customers and improving customer-facing capabilities, a business cannot survive. So the next question might be to understand why customers leave and the role that management has in either preventing that or causing it to happen. If customers leave, there is no one to point the finger to but top management. It's not the customer service agent's fault.

According to the Forum Group, customers leave because (Anton, 1996):

- 45% - of "poor service"
- 20% - of "lack of attention"
- 15% - they found "a better price"
- 15% - they found "a better product"
- 5% - unspecified reasons

There is a serious disconnect between what executives talk about wanting, and what their companies are actually doing. For instance, in research conducted at the Center for Customer Driven-Quality at Purdue University on the annual reports of all publicly owned Fortune 500 companies, there were no firms reporting actual numbers of loyal customers (Anton and Petouhoff, 2002). In most cases, the most important asset, the customer, was not even mentioned! We also found that while 87% of these companies had listed customer satisfaction as one of their most important corporate initiatives, only 16% had any measurement in place to determine they were reaching it. The responsibility to measure customer satisfaction lies with the board of directors providing the executive management team with a strategic objective to measure customer satisfaction. How can a company manage something they don't measure!

In figure 2.1, we can see the evolution of the customer service center. If executives began to look at the customer service center as a business unit unto itself (rather than that department in the basement they don't want to deal with), then it would make sense that there needs to be an evolution in its accompanying business strategy and measurement criteria. This might mean that in this new customer economy, management needs to change what they focus on. There needs to be an accompanying evolution of some of the key aspects in the customer service center and how it is managed, including the

- metrics,
- management,
- technical focus,
- business goals, and
- communications channels.

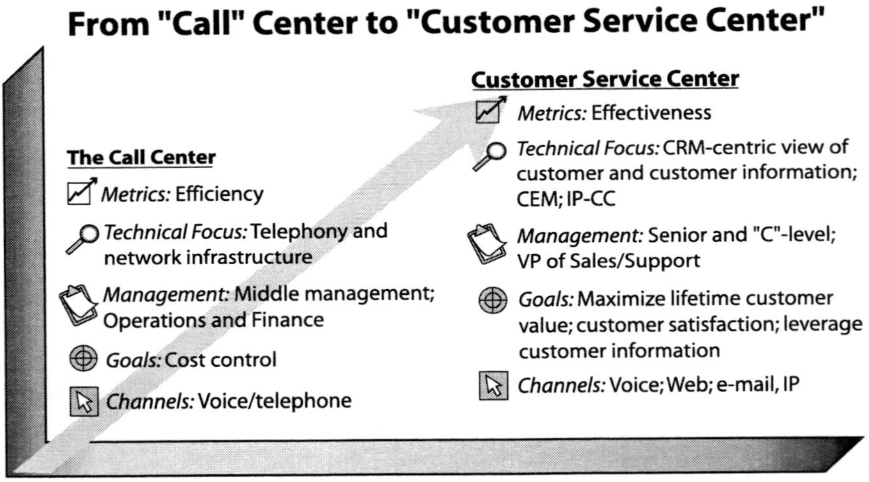

From "Call" Center to "Customer Service Center"

Customer Service Center

☑ *Metrics:* Effectiveness

The Call Center

🔍 *Technical Focus:* CRM-centric view of customer and customer information; CEM; IP-CC

☑ *Metrics:* Efficiency

🔍 *Technical Focus:* Telephony and network infrastructure

📋 *Management:* Senior and "C"-level; VP of Sales/Support

📋 *Management:* Middle management; Operations and Finance

⊕ *Goals:* Maximize lifetime customer value; customer satisfaction; leverage customer information

⊕ *Goals:* Cost control

🔖 *Channels:* Voice/telephone

🔖 *Channels:* Voice; Web; e-mail, IP

Figure 2.1. From call center to customer service center (Aberdeen Group, October 2002)

A key reason for customer service agents not delivering the quality service and sales potential required to be a strategic element in an organization is in the difference in customer service centers' measures for success and the factors that lead to building sales and managing customer relationships.

Customer service center metrics are typically focused on efficiencies: hold times and number of calls handled, to name a few. Even most of the customer-focused measures, such as customer satisfaction, are inaccurate and misleading. As each operation defines their measures in their own way, there is no industry standard or

16

benchmark for customer service center performance. Measures can, and often are, manipulated in order to prove that the customer service center's performance is excellent.

Because these measures are not linked to corporate strategies, they operate in a circular logic: meaningful only to the operations of the customer service center, they are measured against nonsense standards that do not focus on whether the customer service center is meeting the strategic objectives of the organization. Typical efficiency metrics focused on "how many" and "how quickly" creates false hope that all is well, mired down in the false logic that assumes if the customer service center is meeting their efficiency goals, they are also meeting the customers' needs and providing an experience that will build critical relationships.

Customer service agents are your company's listening posts. They are the first to hear when things are going wrong. Want to reduce the number of products that continue to go out your door with missing or defective parts? Want to reduce the number of returned products? Want to know what products people like the most and why? Then review the data in the customer service center and find out what is going on in your business. And do it every single day. Otherwise, if you rely on the reports that come at the end of the month or quarter, your product—and, hence, company—may have reached a point of no return. That could be prevented if executives paid attention to what the customer service agents know. Turning a big ship around is not so hard when you find out quickly that you are off course. Waiting until you've sailed in the wrong direction for months means you mostly likely will end up some place you did not expect.

Previous focus in the technical arena has been on telephony and network infrastructure. In the past, the technology was limited to the communications channels of voice via the telephone. Today, with the emergence of "customer asking," everyone is trying to understand and implement a CRM-centric view of the customer and the customer's information using dozens of types of technology. The customer now expects to be able to contact to the company via many more channels, including voice, Web, e-mail, fax, kiosk and PDAs. All these new technological changes place added stress and requirements on customer service agents. They must learn how to use this equipment and use it well, in order for you to get your investment back. Have you ever used the software they use? You might want to try it. You'd be surprised at what they are required to learn and become proficient at.

As we discussed in Chapter 1, transformation is underway to align the business goals and objectives of the customer service center with the company's corporate objectives. Previous goals of cost control are shifting away from mass management and handle time to meaningful customer-centric metrics such as

- managing customer value,
- measuring customer satisfaction,
- leveraging customer information, and
- managing the customer experience.

However, today's customer service centers fall short of expectations because the evolution of the customer service center is not complete. They are close, but they have not quite reached the pinnacle of their capabilities. Why is this? The rapid rate of business change, coupled with new products coming to market faster than ever; constantly changing workforce; companies merging at record speed; and globalization being a fact of life contribute to the complexities of the customer service center. As customer expectations become more demanding, ensuring that customer service agents can effectively handle complex inquiries is now more critical than ever.

Long gone are the days when a company could take the time—an average of 18-24 months—to train customer service agents to be the best they could be. It worked because products and services were stable. They did not change much and market conditions were more predictable.

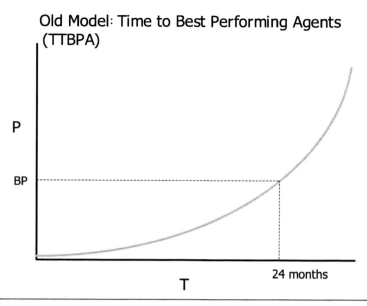

Figure 2.2. Old Model: Time to Best Performing Agents

Today, it's a different and difficult world. The fact that the business world is ever-changing is now so true that it has become a cliché. With every twist and turn, every change in positioning, strategy and product/service mix, the customer service agent is the key person communicating and informing the customer.

The time to best performance needs to be shorter than ever. Companies demand more from their customer service agents today because they have to. The overwhelming challenge and the stay-awake question at night for executives becomes, how quickly can I fill my customer service center with best performers, and how do I keep them performing to customers expectations?

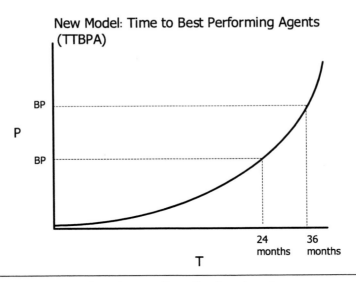

Figure 2.3. New Model: Time to Best Performing Agents

Executives are also coming to realize that with every change that is made to products and services, there is a tremendous burden on the company to keep customer service agents informed. If agents are not informed, it shows in customer loyalty.

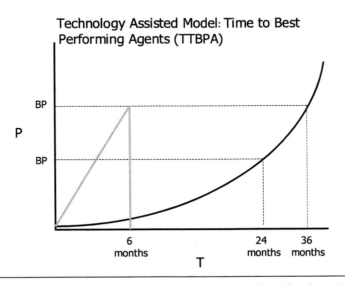

Figure 2.4. Technology Assisted Model: Time to Best Performing Agents

The Customer Service Center: The Corporate Sweet Spot

Organizations have invested billions in technology and process improvements, but ironically, after all that investment, only efficiencies have improved, not effectiveness or performance. Thousands of companies have embraced CRM concepts and technologies during the past decade, often creating impressive benefits. However, companies still face some significant challenges in making their CRM initiatives continue to provide an acceptable return on investment. There is more data available to customer service agents today than ever before. The problem is that they don't know what to do with it. Recently, a customer service agent noted the following: "We have all this great information at our finger tips. The problem is we don't know what finger to use."

- 69% of CRM implementations failed to meet all goals
- 45.3% were late
- 36.8% were over budget
- 31.7% did not produce any meaningful result
  —Selling Power, CSO Forum

The Promise of Self-Service

Self-service is still a growing area. When it is well done, it can be a great channel for providing customer service. If this channel is poorly deployed, it can result in either lost customers or increased calls. While research experts expected customers to take to this lower cost option of delivering service, as we observed in figure 1.5 only 8% of customers use self-service compared to 92% who want to talk to a customer service agent. While for many companies their online presence is a cost reducer, it is not a sales enhancer. This is because lower value transactions are pushed to IVR and Web self-service. However, the higher value transactions are still mainly handled by the customer service agents.

The Promise Of Routing

The promise of enterprise routing was to be able to route your best customer to your best performing agent. However, it is extremely difficult to capture and identify the customer's needs efficiently prior to routing the call. In addition, levels of proficiency or regard for actual performance on calls are not taken into consideration.

21

In some cases, all interactions, voice, e-mail, or the Web are funneled to a universal queue and then routed based on business rules. This precision routing maximizes the productivity of the customer service center resources and allows the company to segment and prioritize customer interactions according to the value of the customer to the company, the desired service level or specific needs (Anton and Vilsoet, 2003). In order to meet the service level goals and real-time traffic, these solutions are able to adjust the size of the assigned customer service agent group according to agent skill levels. Network routing allows companies to maximize customer service center resources by treating distributed centers and customer service agents as one large customer service center. So what is the missing ingredient? "Connect your best agent" assumes that he is capable. The question is "How do they get that way?"

For many companies, the customer service center is the central point for customer interactions, yet Customer Relationship Management (CRM) initiatives have been primarily focused on other customer-facing business units within an organization. And even though today's number one business objective for organizations is to increase customer retention and value, companies continue to view their customer service centers as low-level complaint-takers rather than a mission-critical workforce with the ability to directly impact the bottom line. Because of this, companies miss thousands of opportunities every day to improve customer profitability and retention through the customer service center. Every moment-of-truth counts when you are dealing with customers (Anton, 1997). Most of us can recall the two or three experiences with customer service agents where they exceeded our expectations. This, by itself, describes the general level of satisfaction. Thank goodness for acceptable indifference.

In figure 2.5, we can see that a customer's perception can fall into one of three categories, better than expected, as expected and less than expected (Anton and deRuyter, 1991). And with these perceptions are satisfaction levels. If companies focused on the gap in customer perception versus expectation as shown in figure 2.6, all that CRM technology might start to pay off (Anton and Petouhoff, 2002).

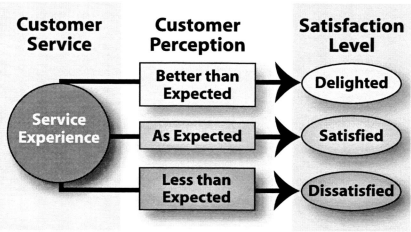

Figure 2.5. Customer service versus customer perception and satisfaction

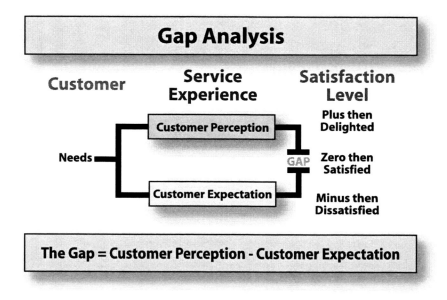

Figure 2.6. The gap between customer perception versus expectation

The key to leveraging this critical link between an executive's strategic vision and the reality of your customers' experience is to view customer service agents as a strategic organizational asset and directly link their performance to corporate objectives.

The Conflicting Priorities of the Modern Customer Service Center

Transforming customer contacts into solid relationships can provide organizations with a significant competitive differentiator. Yet lack of product knowledge in a changing environment, limited ability to manage calls, inadequate communication skills, high absenteeism and turnover, and failure to link corporate objectives of sales and revenue plague this critical link.

Customer service management has focused on efficiency without an accompanying focus on effectiveness (Anton and Gustin, 2000). As a result, agent performance issues largely prevent organizations from reaching the pinnacle of their capabilities. Are efficiency and effectiveness friends or foes? Can management change their old mindset to incorporate both? Where did the focus on efficiency come from? Let's look at what each of these words mean with respect to customer service agents.

Agent efficiency is accomplishing assigned tasks with a minimum of resources. Efficiency measurements include:

- hold time,
- handle time,
- service level,
- cost per call, and more.

Agent effectiveness really boils down to the agents doing the right thing at the right time. Effectiveness measurements include:

- sales close ratios,
- revenue per shift,
- customer satisfaction,
- customer loyalty,
- first-call resolution, and more.

Management's Role In Achieving the Fundamental Mission

Customer service centers are comprised of calls, people and data. Studies have shown that the investments made in the customer service center are represented as follows:

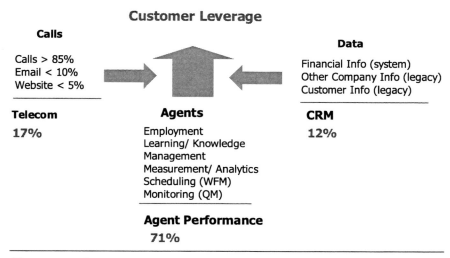

Customer Leverage

Calls

Calls > 85%
Email < 10%
Website < 5%

Telecom

17%

Data

Financial Info (system)
Other Company Info (legacy)
Customer Info (legacy)

Agents

Employment
Learning/ Knowledge
Management
Measurement/ Analytics
Scheduling (WFM)
Monitoring (QM)

CRM

12%

Agent Performance

71%

Figure 2.7. Investments have focused on data and technology, not on making people better.

For too long, companies have made significant technological investments to improve customer service and have ignored the human performance element that directly impacts customer loyalty. As companies are continuously challenged not only to deliver more sophisticated sales and service capabilities, but also to manage these capabilities more quickly and cost effectively, executives will eventually conclude that they only way to compete effectively is to fill customer service centers with more best performers—faster.

> ## Handle Time versus Customer Satisfaction
>
> One of the big debates, for instance, in customer service centers is about handle time. An extreme, but not uncommon example was unveiled in a recent Harvard Business Review article, in which a customer service center's "Platinum" line, dedicated to a leading airline's best customers, automatically disconnected callers who had been on hold for 59 minutes. When asked why the system did that, the manager admitted that he was compensated on the average time required to handle customers' calls – including the time spent on hold. Hanging up on callers was the only way to hit his targets. Ironically, while this airline's customer service center was hanging up on their top-tier customers, the organization's corporate objectives centered around becoming more customer-focused and differentiating themselves on the quality of customer service.
>
> —*Bridging the Gap Between Executive Vision and Agent Performance*, 2002.

Similarities To Manufacturing

Customer service centers can be considered the factory floor of our generation. What did manufacturing focus on? They focused on efficiency: speed, cost reductions...and more.

Are we repeating a pattern without thinking it through? Productivity has long been the most important customer service center success criteria, with customer service agents typically judged by the quantity of their daily contacts, not the quality of how they interact with callers. The reasoning seems sound: the more productive the agents, the fewer agents required. The result: lower operating costs. But what is the price tag for these reduced operating costs? Too often, customer dissatisfaction, lost sales opportunities, and customer defections. By stressing speed over quality of service experience, an organization is practically guaranteed that their customer service agents will frustrate their customers instead of helping them.

Let's consider the following timeline:

Manufacturing	Customer Service
• **1901 – Introduction of the assembly line.**	· 1973 – Rockwell introduced the ACD.
· 1960's – Responding to poor quality, American manufacturers added inspectors to do post-production random inspections.	· 1988 – Responding to poor quality, Technekron introduced quality monitoring for post-production random inspections.
· ~1980 – Responding to economic pressure, American manufacturers re-think quality, focus on building quality in (TQM) · ~1990 – Realizing economic benefit, American manufacturers embrace six sigma and focus on getting variability out.	Customer service does not meet anyone's expectations. Executives in search of transformation will focus on building quality in and getting variability out.

Figure 2.8. Similarities of the customer service center and manufacturing

Not only are typical customer service center metrics driving actions that run counter to corporate strategy and objectives, they often provide little quality data to executives. Customer service center measures focused on efficiency do not provide executives with information that can improve product quality, save corporate costs, increase revenues or change business relationships with customers—issues that are of strategic significance to the entire organization. The most important thing that management can do is to articulate clear objectives for the modern customer service center. Then set performance goals and expectations against those objectives. This means translating performance goals into measurable metrics that the center can strive to achieve.

CHAPTER 3: PROFILE OF AMERICANS THAT CALL COMPANIES

Your customer service center is a key contributor to your corporate image and to your repeat business. Ground-breaking research study, described in this chapter, shows why every executive should be concerned about the competitive performance of his or her customer service center operations (Anton, Rockwell and Setting, 2003).

This chapter presents a graphical presentation of the answers that respondents gave to a survey of key demographics and psychographics of Americans that contact company customer service centers. This study was conducted by our research staff in June 2002, sponsored by Kelly Services (the complete white paper is available at <www.BenchmarkPortal.com>).

Impact of Customer Service Centers on Company Image

The purpose of this research was to survey a statistical sample of the American population to determine their perception of the level of customer service provided by companies over the telephone, also known as "customer service center." The survey correlates these perceptions with their "image" of the company and their propensity to spend more money with that company in the future. The results of this study were aimed, in particular, at customer service center managers and senior executives.

Demographics of the Respondents

- The majority are between 26 and 55 years old.
- More than 50 percent have at least a four-year college degree.
- The average income is more than $50,000 per year.

Most Important Findings Articulated by the American Respondents

1. Seventy-two percent of the respondents felt the call handling experience "met their expectations;" however, "meeting expectations" was not enough to improve their intentions to "repurchase" the company's products and/or services.

2. More than 75 percent of the respondents that reported the call "exceeded their expectations" felt this would influence

29

them to purchase the company's product and/or services again.

3. Sixty-three percent of the respondents that reported the call was a "bad experience" felt they would stop using the company's products or services as a result.

4. Ninety-two percent of the respondents reported that the call experience influenced their "image" of the company they had called.

5. Eighty-one percent of the respondents reported that the issue about which they called was handled on the first call.

6. If the call was to resolve a complaint and the caller deemed the experience unsatisfactory, the likelihood of that caller severing the relationship with the company was almost double that of a non-complaint call.

7. There was a significant positive correlation between handling the caller's issue on the first call and a response of "exceeded my expectations."

Additional Findings Articulated by the American Respondents

1. The majority of respondents had called a company within the past two weeks.

2. The primary reason for calling the company was to ask for help and/or information.

3. The vast majority of respondents had no problem finding the toll-free number for the company's customer service center.

The results of this study confirmed that the customer service center experience has a significant impact on how customers perceive a company's image and brand, and on how likely they are to repurchase products or services from that company. This indicates that companies would be prudent to view their customer service centers as a crucial element of their customer strategy, akin to marketing and loyalty programs. It also suggests that it is imperative to monitor customer satisfaction on a regular basis.

The Respondent's Perception of Their Call

In this section, we graphically depict the answers that respondents gave to each question related to their **experience** in contacting a customer service center. Each of the questions had at least two possible answers. For each question, the percentage of respondents who answered each option is displayed in one of the following graphs. The following shows how the respondent's replies were divided among the possible answers to each question.

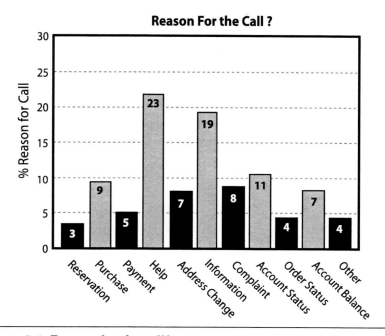

Figure 3.1. Reason for the call?

Question: What was the reason for your last call to a company?

Finding: Figure 3.1 shows the various reasons that the participants called a customer service center, and the frequency in percent of how the participants responded. As you can see, "request for help with a product or service" was the most popular reason for the call at 23 percent of the total, with "request for information" a close second at 19 percent of the total call reasons.

Interpretation: Accessibility to information and assistance through the telephone has become a "feature" expected by American consumers of every product and service. The customer service center can be an effective channel to deliver this important feature.

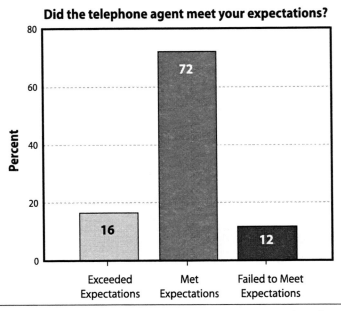

Did the telephone agent meet your expectations?

Figure 3.2. Did the telephone agent meet your expectations?

Question: In your most recent experience in calling for customer service assistance, how did the telephone agent do in satisfying your needs and handling your call?

Finding: Figure 3.2 shows responses to whether the caller felt the manner in which the representative handled the call exceeded, met, or failed to meet expectations.

Respondents who indicated their expectations were "met" or "exceeded" were asked the next question in the survey. Those whose experience "failed to meet" expectations skipped the next question.

As the graph shows, a significantly smaller percentage of people's expectations were "exceeded" than "met."

Interpretation: Only when companies exceed expectations do customers become more loyal and therefore more likely to repurchase from the company. Since only 16 percent reported "exceeded expectations," we conclude there is significant room for improvement in customer service centers to "delight" the caller.

After Good Experience Would Use Company in Future

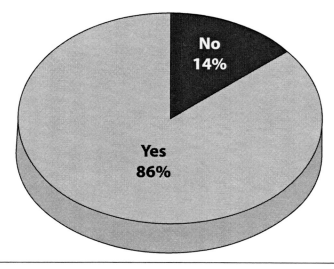

Figure 3.3. After good experience, would use company in future

Question: Based on this positive experience, will you use this company in preference over their competitors in the future?

Finding: Figure 3.3 shows the results of only those respondents who said that their call handling experience either "met" or "exceeded" their expectations. As you can see, most said they would use the company again in the future.

Interpretation: With the overwhelming response being "yes," it is clear to us that a caller's experience with a customer service center definitely impacts his/her loyalty and willingness to repurchase.

After Bad Experience, Would Stop Using Company in Future

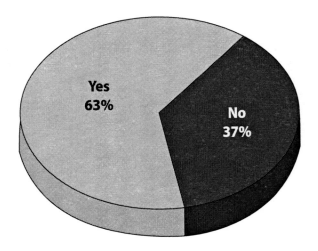

Figure 3.4. After bad experience, would stop using company in future

Question: Based on this negative experience, will you stop using this company in preference to their competitors in the future?

Finding: Figure 3.4 shows the results only for those respondents who indicated that the call handling had "not met their expectations". As you can see, the majority of participants would move to a competitor after their bad experience with the customer service center.

Interpretation: We believe that those who had a bad calling experience, but indicated they would not stop using the company's product in the future, probably found it too difficult or time-consuming to make the switch. We have found in other studies that when it is easy to switch to a competitor, consumers do so. When switching takes time and effort or expense, they are more hesitant.

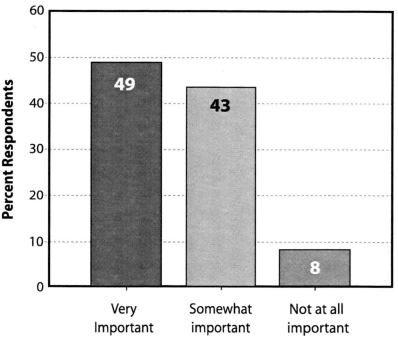

How important was your overall call experience in shaping your image of the company?

Figure 3.5. How did experience shape image of the company?

Question: How important was your overall call experience in shaping your overall image of this company?

Finding: As you can see in figure 3.5, the overwhelming majority of participants (49 percent plus 43 percent) felt their call experience was important in shaping their image of the company.

Interpretation: We feel this is a critical finding. It proves our initial hypothesis that since customer service centers are often the most frequent point of personal contact with a company, they are responsible for a major part of the branding and image of that company. We feel that top executives already have a "gut feel" that this is the case, and with this finding will be more willing to do whatever it takes to make the customer service center a strategic differentiator for the company.

The Respondents' Demographics

In this section, we explored the basic demographics of the respondents.

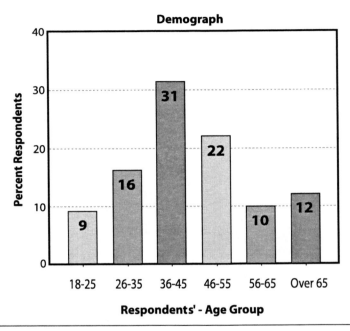

Figure 3.6. Respondents' demographics

Question: Which age group do you belong to?

Finding: In figure 3.6 we see the frequency of various age groupings in our research that use the telephone to contact companies. As was expected, the majority of the respondents were in the age range of 26 to 55 years old, with the peak group being between 36 and 45 years old.

Interpretation: This is an important finding for companies with a customer service center. The age range from 36 to 45 is certainly a group of Americans that companies want to attract and service properly, since this age group is the most active in contacting companies for assistance and for information. It is also an age group with growing disposable income and purchasing power.

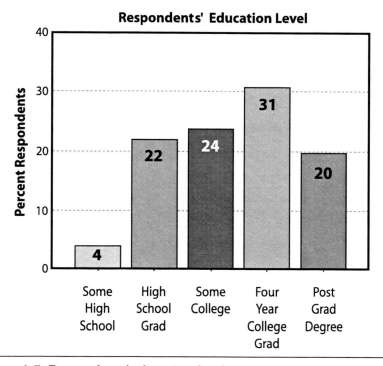

Figure 3.7. Respondents' education level

Question: What is your level of education?

Finding: Figure 3.7 shows there is an even spread between high school graduates and college-educated respondents. Seventy-five percent of the respondents have at least some college education, and 51 percent of the respondents have four or more years of college education.

Interpretation: In our opinion, the demographics and psychographics of the population that most companies target their products to is the same group that is most likely to call the toll-free number for assistance and/or for information. This is an important finding that should motivate companies to make sure their customer service center is all that it can be in delivering superb quality service to this kind of educated customer.

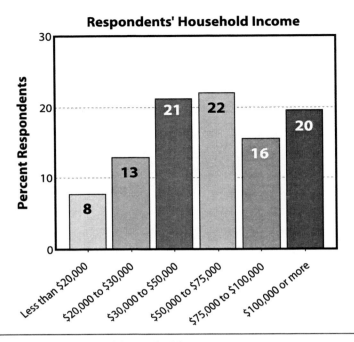

Figure 3.8. Respondents' household income

Question: Please share with us your annual income.

Finding: Figure 3.8 shows the distribution of annual household income for the respondents. Eighty percent are in the "$30,000+" per year bracket. Fifty-eight percent are in the "$50,000+" per year bracket.

Interpretation: The importance of this finding for companies is to emphasize that the typical American calling a customer service center has substantial annual income and buying power and future purchasing influence.

Will you use this company in preference over competitors?

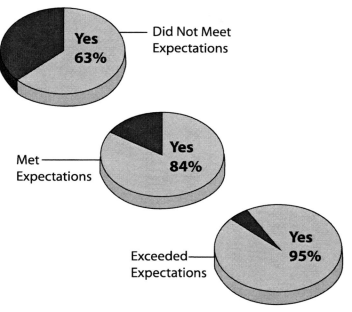

Figure 3.9. Use company in preference over competitors?

Questions: 1. In your most recent experience in calling for customer service assistance, how did the telephone agent do in satisfying your needs and handling your call?

2. Based on this positive experience, will you use this company in preference over their competitors in the future?

Finding: In figure 3.9, we see an interesting correlation between "exceeding expectations" and the percentage of participants who would use the company again in the future. As you can see, a greater percentage of respondents whose expectations were "exceeded" said they would use the company again versus those whose expectations were only "met."

Interpretation: Figure 3.9 shows that the customer must receive "wow" service to help ensure his/her loyalty and intention to repurchase.

Keep in mind this graph also shows that 16 percent of the people whose expectations were "met" would not use the company again in the future—this is a crucial finding for customer service center managers striving for quality.

Would Use Company in the Future?

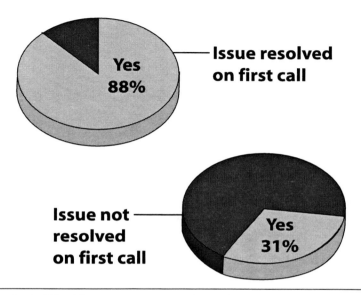

Figure 3.10. Would use company in future?

Questions: 1. Based on this positive experience, will you use this company in preference over their competitors in the future?

2. Was your issue (reason for the call) resolved on the initial contact?

Finding: In figure 3.10, we see that those participants whose issue was resolved on the first call are more likely to use the company again in the future.

Interpretation: As we have seen in every study on this matter, the highest driver of caller satisfaction and willingness to repurchase is the ability to resolve the issue on the first call. For all customer service center managers, this must be the one key performance indicator to follow closely. Doing poorly on this metric is often a clear indicator of systemic problems.

CHAPTER 4: CUSTOMER SERVICE AT A CROSSROADS

The Road Ahead for Today's Customer Service Center

In Chapter 2 we looked at the role of the Board of Directors, executives and middle management. What we learned is that the responsibility for ensuring customer delight begins with these three groups. We also saw that customer service center measurements that focus on efficiency do not provide executives with information that can improve product quality, save corporate costs, increase revenues or change business relationships with customers. What we will learn in this chapter is that customer service is truly at a crossroads. The notable difference when comparing companies who have been successful and those who have not, is to examine the differences in how they made it to the other side. Throughout this chapter, we will examine the modernization of manufacturing and its profound impact on business management around the world. We will also review the findings of service leaders such as Dr. W. Edwards Deming, Dr. Joseph Huran and others.

Performance is achieved by giving customer concerns a top priority. By studying and constantly improving key work processes, the final service product will then be able to meet or exceed the customer expectations. Deming's theory is that as the process improves, the productivity goes up and the inefficiencies go down (Deming, 1986). Customers get better products at lower prices and the company becomes more effective at providing what customers want. Customers who receive high quality products or services tell others causing demand to increase. Deming summarized this cycle in figure 4.1 as the Deming Chain Reaction.

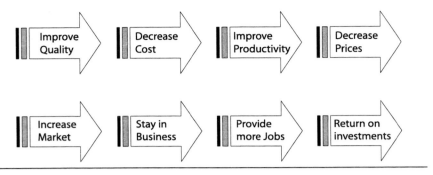

Figure 4.1. The Deming Chain Reaction

Dr. Juran gave us the 85/15 rule (Juran, 1999). At the time of developing his theory the prevailing leadership paradigm was that "A company would have few if any problems if only the workers would do their jobs correctly." What Juran did was prove that the potential to eliminate mistakes and errors lies mostly in improving the systems through which work is done and not by blaming the worker. The rule of thumb is that 85% of problems can only be corrected by changing the systems (which are mostly determined by management) and less than 15% are under a worker's control.

For example, a customer service agent can't do a top quality job if they don't have the knowledge or tools; a surgeon cannot do an excellent job with gloves that do not fit. And even when it does appear that an individual is doing something wrong, more times than not, the trouble lies in how the employee was trained. Training is a systemic problem that can be changed only by management. Juran encouraged management teams to stop blaming the individual workers. Instead he suggested asking themselves, "Which systems need improvement?" to find out the true source of the problem.

What we learned in Chapter 2 is that in order to close the gap between the company and their customers, executives need to fill their customer service centers with more best performers—faster. This means that the customer service center needs a new education process oriented towards effectiveness in order to achieve business goals. The good news is we are starting to get a handle on how to address the root cause issue. And instead of reinventing the wheel, we can turn to an industry we already know a lot about; manufacturing.

Customer Service Center Similarities to Manufacturing

So how is the manufacturing world similar to the customer service center? Manufacturing has discrete products which are made over and over again. Customer service centers are similar in that they have individual calls which are handled over and over. And just like manufacturing that focused for years on efficiency and cost reduction, so have customer service centers. But something occurred in the American manufacturing market that changed all that. It is a lesson that business need best heed than repeat. What happened was shocking. American automakers lost customers and therefore revenue, profits and growth. Why? Partially because of what is called the management by results method of running business (Walton and Deming, 1988).

Management by Results

Management by results is structured by a chain of command and a hierarchy of objectives, goals and accountability (Deming, 2000). The traditional organizational charts portrays a chain of accountability and the performance is guided and judged according to numerical goals. The shortcomings of management by results are rooted in the use of goals to reward and punish. It does not pay attention to the process and systems which define the real capabilities of the organization to reach the goals. So instead of the goals being real, they become arbitrary, and therefore, lead employees, supervisors and managers to play games. "Looking good" overshadows the concern for the work they are supposed to get done. The use of just numerical goals to judge and reward performance fosters a host of problems that creates more problems (Walton and Deming, 1988). These problems include

- short-term thinking,
- internal conflicts,
- fudging numbers and results,
- increasing fear of losing a job, and
- blindness to customer concerns.

Short-term thinking means the near horizon gets attention. Top managers impose goals on lower managers, who impose goals on employees. Employees struggle to meet the goals and in the struggle they become too busy meeting quotas to even care about customers. When these goals are met, the entire company boasts of its performance. But if the truth be known, this attitude wreaks havoc with quality, employee morale and customer satisfaction.

45

Systems of numerical controls cause internal conflicts. An example is when salespeople make promises other areas can't keep. Designers rush new products into production too quickly. The conflicts lead to finger pointing, blame games and endless series of excuses... "If it weren't for them...we could..." Each group struggles to meet goals independent of each other and turf wars flourish.

With respect to fudging numbers and results, as we saw in Chapter 2 with the story of the airline customer service center manager disconnecting callers who had been on hold for 59 minutes to meet his quotas, we see that imposed measurable goals are many times unattainable. That is because they lie about the system's capability. Since employees don't want to fail, they lie to make it look like they are conforming. The system encourages them to fudge figures, alter records, or just "play the game" to work around the system instead of improving it.

> "There is no excuse to offer for putting people on a job that they know not how to do. Most so-called 'goofing off'—somebody seems to be lazy, doesn't seem to care—that person is almost always in the wrong job, or has very poor management."
>
> –Deming

One of the worst fall-outs from management by results is fear. Employees fear what will happen if the commands are not followed exactly. They might lose face, not get a promotion or raise or worse yet, they might get fired. The more rigid and unrealistic the controls, the deeper the fear in the organization, the more in-the-box thinking occurs (Petouhoff and Koons, 2003).

> "People are entitled to joy in their work and a sense of ownership."
>
> –Deming

And last but not least is the customer. Management by results encourages a company to look inward, rather than outward where the customer is. Expecting a company to become customer facing when the management and reward system is internally driven is ludicrous. Accomplishments in a management-by-results company come from meeting a numerical goal, rather than in providing a product or service that works and satisfies the customer.

You can begin to see how all these problems compound one another. Can you see your organization operating in any of these ways? What is the impact? In most companies, people think they are doing a good job by trying to meet the organization's internal standards. However, these organizational standards driven by management by results provide a Titanic-like false sense of security. When people realize that what they are focusing on is the wrong thing, the ship is already sinking.

The parallel in the customer service center is getting all customer-facing operations and systems to work in coordination. Customers will not stand for the purgatory of being transferred around an organization to have multiple questions answered: they want the person who picks up the phone to be the sole point of contact. To satisfy customer needs, organizations are combining different customer-facing activities into their customer service centers, so that one agent might handle service, support, order processing and inside sales. In fact, nearly 65% of respondents in a recent Aberdeen study indicated that they were working on complete integration of their customers service centers with other customer-facing activities.

Management in America Evolves for Awhile and Then Regresses

The production demands of World War II led to the creation of innovative approaches to improving productivity and quality in the manufacturing of military goods. Statistical process control (SPC) and worker involvement were widely used (Shewhart and Deming, 1986). Workers, now more widely educated than workers of twenty or thirty years earlier, were able to plan their work as well as do it; they also checked the quality, and improved both product quality and work processes.

After the war, U.S. manufacturers shifted focus to rapidly fulfill pent-up consumer demand from ten years of economic depression and five years of war. The emphasis was on quantity, not quality, or getting a high volume of product out the door as quickly as possible. The vast majority of the systems and qualitative workplace innovations developed during the war were abandoned.

A reason for shifting away from the newly learned systems and process design was due to lack of focus from senior management. During the war senior management had not learned the new planning and management methods their companies employed; the

47

people who learned it were at lower levels in the company. After the war senior management did what they always do, take charge; engineers once again planned, managers once again exercised command and control authority, and workers once again were just expected to do the work, and quality control inspectors would check the work after it was done.

Senior managers in Japan learned quality and systems thinking from Americans and then improved even more (Aguayo and Deming, 1991). After World War II, Japan needed to rebuild its economy, literally from the ground up. They were taught by Americans to use the same kinds of successful process management and systems thinking used by U.S. industry during the war. Under direction from General Douglas MacArthur, teams taught the Japanese senior management how to manage modern manufacturing factories. It was an eight week course that ran eight-hours a day, four days a week.

In 1950, W. Edwards Deming began teaching statistical process administration to get better results in manufacturing (Aguayo and Deming, 1991). He also taught new philosophies of process, quality, and systems thinking that proved so successful in American industry during the war. The goal was to view mass production as an interdependent system, use statistics to analyze what the system is doing and get it under control, eliminate waste, and drive costs down. At a minimum you get the benefit of not spending money and time fixing mistakes. In 1954 Joseph Juran went to Japan and introduced continuous improvement ideas, stressing breakthroughs, project teams, and annual improvement.

In the early 1960s quality and continuous improvement philosophy spread in Japan to first-line supervisors with the publication of Ishikawa's materials in the Foreman Magazine on the Seven Tools for Quality Control. This began the integration of the techniques and philosophy into the daily work life of the Japanese factory worker. In the mid-1960s Komatsu Tractor applied continuous improvement principles to the entire company in the form of Total Quality Control (TQC).

In the early 1970s Japanese industrialists began the application of TQC principles to the "front-end" of the business of understanding the customer. They developed a tool called Quality Function Deployment (QFD) to get the voice of the customer in a statistically significant way and build that into their planning and production system. They also expanded the Shewhart/Deming Cycle beyond R&D

to include marketing, sales, engineering, quality, and manufacturing (Shewhart and Deming, 1986). In the mid-1970s the Arab oil crisis caused resource-sensitive Japan to redouble its TQC efforts in manufacturing while expanding its efforts in the service sector.

The Impact in the United States

In the late 1970s many American manufacturers suddenly discovered that the slowly building loss of customers had now become a serious threat to their existence. The customers were buying Japanese products that were of better quality at lower prices (Aguayo and Deming, 1991). American industry had first tried to compete by reducing employees and by moving factories to find lower cost employees. Some communities, especially in the northeast and midwest, were suffering from serious job losses.

In the early 1980s American senior management thought the Japanese government was subsidizing industry because they did not believe it was possible to produce such high quality products, and sell them profitably at the prices they were charging. They wanted the U.S. government to retaliate and protect them. We learned from Dr. Deming that American business was using faulty leadership and management theories and methods. This was causing their companies to produce poor quality products, experience high costs, and fail to please their customers. In the 1950s, 1960s, and the first half of the 1970s, American companies got away with poor quality and high prices because the consumer had no alternatives. That changed in the second half of the 1970s when the consumer discovered high quality Japanese goods at attractive prices.

American managers now found themselves in serious trouble as sales dropped to dangerous levels. They were now anxious to learn how the Japanese industrialists were able to do this. In late 1983 four GOAL/QPC leaders (Bob King, Diane Ritter, Charles McCarthy, and Laurence Smith), armed with a letter of introduction from Dr. Deming, made a study trip to JUSE in Tokyo (Aguayo and Deming, 1991). JUSE was the organization that coordinated Dr. Deming's work in the 1950s. The group brought back a great deal of knowledge about the tools and methods of Japanese TQC.

Does History Have to Repeat Itself?

Deming was initially ignored in the United States. But the war-battered Japanese took a deep interest in his statistical methods, which eliminated inspections and made quality everybody's job. Deming didn't catch on in the United States until 1981, after NBC aired a documentary titled "If Japan Can, Why Can't We?" Deming was invited to Ford by Don Peterson (Aguayo and Deming, 1991).

> Deming ripped apart Ford's quality effort. Deming's number one concern: Ford relied on inspections rather than building products right the first time.

Ford stated, "He has so much to offer. It's so awful that this country didn't tap into him years ago." What Deming teaches is that managers, not workers, are responsible for 80% of the defects in products or a service. The workers aren't bad; the system is bad.

Lessons From Manufacturing

Deming's methods work in service companies, too. As we analyzed the customer service center, we became fascinated with the efficiency focus with the advent of the ACD. We saw the ACD as the customer service center equivalent of the assembly line. We also became concerned about "product" quality. The inspection process was put at the end of the "line" (after the product was already built) i.e., quality monitoring and customer surveys. This was similar to what happened in the American Auto Industry; inspecting quality in rather than building it in.

> "Inspection with the aim of finding the bad ones and throwing them out is too late, ineffective, costly. Quality comes not from inspection but from improvement of the process."
>
> —Deming

Ultimately, manufacturers learned that greater consistency in output is achieved when quality is integrated into the manufacturing process, not punitively fixed after the product is manufactured. The integration of quality in manufacturing came in the form of greater emphasis on, and expectations from, human performance. This is also the case in the customer service center (Fleischer, 2001). With the goal of creating a more satisfying experience for their customers—and boosting customer loyalty and retention—many customer service centers have invested huge sums and effort into deploying customer relationship management (CRM) systems. Unfortunately, many of these same customer service centers still fail to understand that a CRM solution is only as good as the people who use it.

Ultimately customer service centers are in search of a way to stamp our variability—to ensure the customer experience is superior, consistent and predictable.

Stamping Out Variability

Variance is the enemy of manufacturing (Shewhart and Deming, 1986). Product variance creates cost: re-work, returns, lost customers, poor reputation, poor customer loyalty, and poor financial performance. Like manufacturing, variance is the enemy of the customer service center. Customer service agents execute five to ten discrete processes repeatedly, each individualized to the business and its product and service mix. Getting the agent-to-agent variance out of those processes *is the key to optimizing agent performance and enhancing customer service center profits*. Some understanding of variation, including appreciation of a stable system, and some understanding of special causes and common causes of variation, are essential for management of a system, including the management of people. Deming created a four-part system:

1. appreciation for a system
2. knowledge about variation
3. theory of knowledge
4. psychology

He felt managers needed to understand that all people are different. This is not ranking people. And lastly Deming felt that variation and how people are managed could not be separated.

Differences From Manufacturing

So what are the differences between the customer service center and manufacturing? The "raw material" (the customer) is unpredictable. The customer service agent is required to take the "product" (the call) from start to finish. In manufacturing more than one product is manufactured during a given period (day). Customer service agents, as we previously stated, execute five to ten discrete processes repeatedly. The "product" (call) affects the customer relationship in real-time. Re-work is not an option. And while re-work is not an option in a good manufacturing process, generally the rework is done before the customer gets the product. In customer service centers, rework is not possible because the customer has defected.

The Big "AH HA"

Unlike manufacturing, in the customer service center, agent performance is the _only_ way to build quality in and get variability out. While manufacturing is product-focused, the customer service center is people-oriented. There is heavier emphasis placed on people and their performance to meet customer expectations. This is because

- the "raw material" (the customer) is unpredictable,
- the customer service agent is expected to take a variety of differing "products" (call) from start to finish, and
- the "product" (call) affects the customer relationship in real-time.

Customer service agents simply have to perform. Routing strategies and data aggregation cannot fix any of the above problems. If agent performance is the _only_ way to build quality in and get variance out, agent performance must be enhanced and it must be enhanced quickly.

Have We Defined Quality Incorrectly?

Quality is defined as value and reliability at a reasonable price. Quality is relentlessly pursued through products and services that delight the customer and through effective and efficient methods of implementation. Work is not haphazard, but it has structure to how it gets done. The structure or process is studied, measured, analyzed and improved.

Quality is not a random inspection. It is not volume forecasting. Quality is not the intersection of calls and data that drives customer loyalty. It is not faster routing nor the routing of more data faster. Quality is purposeful and proactive. More importantly, it is people-focused.

Since 85% of an organization's failures are related to the faults of over-controlled management systems, the focus is on constant and rigorous improvement of every system. Not on blaming individuals. Organizations no longer have barriers, rivalries or distrust. Instead the organization is built around teamwork and collaboration. The teamwork's theme is focused on winning more customers. And the last but most important aspect is that everyone in the organization is constantly learning. Management encourages employees to constantly elevate their skills and knowledge. Employees gain a mastery of their jobs and broaden their capabilities. Management leads by example.

> "Everybody here has a customer. And if he doesn't know who it is and what constitutes the needs of the customer...then he does not understand his job."
> —Deming

Deming's 14 Points

1. Create constancy of purpose toward improvement of product and service, with the aim to become competitive and to stay in business, and to provide jobs.

2. Adopt the new philosophy. We are in a new economic age. Western management must awaken to the challenge, must learn their responsibilities, and take on leadership for change.

3. Cease dependence on inspection to achieve quality. Eliminate the need for inspection on a mass basis by building quality into the product in the first place!!

4. End the practice of awarding business on the basis of price tag. Instead, minimize total cost. Move toward a single supplier for any one item, on a long-term relationship of loyalty and trust.

5. Improve constantly and forever the system of production and service, to improve quality and productivity, and thus constantly decrease costs.

6. Institute training on the job!!

7. Institute leadership. The aim of supervision should be to help people and machines and gadgets do a better job. Supervision of management is in need of overhaul as well as supervision of production workers.

8. Drive out fear, so that everyone may work effectively for the company.

9. Break down barriers between departments. People in research, design, sales, and production must work as a team to foresee problems of production and in use that may be encountered with the product or service.

10. Eliminate slogans, exhortations, and targets for the work force asking for zero defects and new levels of productivity. Such exhortations only create adversarial relationships, as the bulk of the causes of low quality and low productivity belong to the system and thus lie beyond the power of the work force.

11a. Eliminate work standards (quotas) on the factory floor. Substitute leadership.

11b. Eliminate management by objective. Eliminate management by numbers, numerical goals. Substitute leadership.

12a. Remove barriers that rob the hourly worker of his right to joy of workmanship. The responsibility of supervisors must be changed from sheer numbers to quality.

12b. Remove barriers that rob people in management and in engineering of their right to joy of workmanship. This means abolishment of the annual merit rating management by objective.

13. Institute a vigorous program of education and self-improvement.

14. Put everybody in the company to work to accomplish the transformation. The transformation is everybody's job.

—From *OUT OF THE CRISIS* by W. Edwards Deming

CHAPTER 5: QUALITY INTO THE PRODUCT IN THE FIRST PLACE

Falling Into The Gap

In today's fiercely competitive environment we are all looking for improved financial performance. But in the obsession with strategic alignment, mergers and acquisitions, new partners and "e"-enabling processes, many executives have missed a fundamental point; a critically important point. Many organizations have the false sense that they are faring well with their customer service center operations.

According to studies done at the Purdue University Center for Customer-Driven Quality, while 70 percent of enterprises believe they have a well-run customer service center that provides their customers with good service, only 46 percent of customers report satisfaction with that service. This type of gap between the organization's perception and the customer's reality can be devastating to an organization's ability to meet their financial goals and obligations to their shareholders. In many organizations, they have fallen into this gap that represents a chasm within which many customers plummet and are lost to an organization forever.

So what is this gap? Because if we understood this critical gap, then we would be motivated to do everything we can to close it, right? This gap or the weakest link in corporate strategies is the performance of their customer service agents; the very people who represent the company to customers day in and day out.

Have we thought about the customer service agent's role in achieving the fundamental mission of the customer service center? And if so, what are we doing to maximize it? It is important because they are the resource between the company and the customer. However, many times they are not only unable but often unwilling to get the job done right. This can make meeting the expectations of the financial community, the shareholders, and the board quite difficult.

Who's in Charge of the Company's Most Important Asset, the Customer?

The individual who has the most interactions with customers is also typically the most underpaid and under-trained employee in the company. To do their job effectively, the customer service agent must be an expert on multiple products, a psychologist, a skilled politician, a technologist and have a greater depth and breadth of understanding the company, its services and its vision than just about any other employee in the organization. In spite of the requirement for customer service agents to be corporate "renaissance employees," most organizations run their customer service center operations like an assembly line, focusing only on speed, cost reductions and remedial coaching.

In addition, customer service agents do not like their jobs, by and large. Everyone likes to succeed in his or her job—it is human nature to want to have some measure of control over the outcome of your efforts. Yet, there is no visible career path for agents, so they often feel like migrant farm labors. With the lack of career goals and dealing with angry customers, agents do not feel that they are succeeding on a daily basis. How much would a nurse like her job if every third patient died on the operating table?

Improving agent performance should be a number one priority to close the gap. By aligning the mission of the customer service center with corporate objectives, it will allow executives to more effectively meet their strategic and financial goals. Sounds simple, right? But if it were simple, then the gap wouldn't exist.

Filling a customer service center with best performers is the only way to achieve customer loyalty goals. Why? Because business has changed and it will continue to change. New business growth was once the mantra and sales force automation the strategy. Business thinkers believed the best path to market domination and enviable margins was through automating the field sales force. Ironically, after automating the process, only efficiencies improved, not business performance. Executives are now discovering the futility of speeding the sales process when the outcome continues to be negative. Customer service centers have similar transaction efficiency focus.

The crisis we find ourselves in is that in order to grow business, customer retention is key. According to a recent Accenture study of 500 global business executives, 80 percent said "people" issues are the most important to achieve growth. However, 36 percent reported there still isn't enough attention being paid to such issues.

Now that customer retention has become the new business focus with a healthy emphasis on the acquisition of profitable customers, the customer service center—more specifically, the customer service agent—will be the strategic asset to leverage. More than ever, a company's destiny will be determined on how well and how fast it can respond to improving performance.

Addressing the customer service center's performance requirements through the same lens, as the rest of the organization will prove unsuccessful. The customer service center is a unique environment and with that come unique requirements for building best performers. Attempting to force fit performance optimization strategies into the customer service center will result in disastrous results. In the next sections we will look at some of the issues surrounding performance improvement of customer service agents and how best to achieve desired results.

Problem #1: The Business World Has Changed

The important trends that defined business in the 90's— globalization, deregulation, and extraordinary technological change— made the decade's countless customer-facing programs both a way for corporations to show they cared about customers and a strategic and operating imperative.

Now, businesses faces new challenges. Executives are caught between heightened pressure from financial markets to increase revenue and reduce costs on the one hand, and increased customer demand for new and enhanced services on the other.

In a world where investment and operational dollars will remain scarce, a more profitable approach to getting and serving customers requires comprehensive strategies that both reduce the cost of service delivery and improve the value of customer interactions.

Agent performance initiatives are disconnected from business objectives (figure 5.1). We do spend resources to improve customer service agent performance, but we do it like the pilgrims did it, with minimal resources. That is because performance goals conflict with operational goals. Operational pressures keep new hire training, and recurrent classroom time to a minimum. Many feel that customer service agents aren't delivering value to the organization if they are sitting in a classroom. Customer service agents are hired to be on the phones with customers. However, at the same time, customer service agents can't deliver value to the organization if they do not have the knowledge and skills to manage customer relationships effectively.

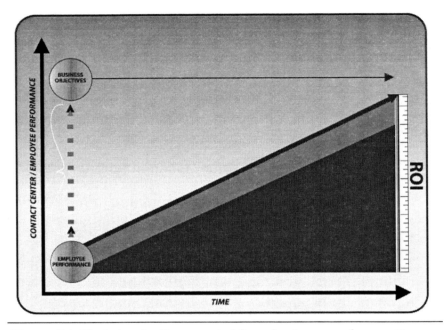

Figure 5.1. Training is disconnected from business goals, creating an overall performance gap in the business

Problem #2: Leakage

The human brain naturally forgets most of what it learns. While few in management would believe that a day of classroom training translates into instant proficiency, most executives would be shocked to realize that up to 80 percent of their training investment is lost within 48 hours of training without proper reinforcement (Robinson, 1989). This means that it's natural for customer service agents to develop knowledge and skill gaps once they go live with customers on the phone. This results in

- inconsistent customer experiences, and
- missed revenue opportunities.

58

Quality monitoring only catches a small fraction of problems. Continuously reinforcing knowledge and skills is, therefore, a critical success factor in managing customer experiences.

Problem #3: Individualization

Knowledge and skill gaps are an issue because they are individualized (figure 5.2). If everyone forgot the same things, then we would train everyone on the things that everyone forgets. It's hard to identify skill gaps from individual to individual. So delivering the right training to specific individuals is key in order to continue to grow the knowledge and skills of individuals.

What training programs also typically fail to take into account are the individualized skill gaps and knowledge that will lead to improved performance for a particular customer service agent. Why insist that each agent go through a huge product refresher course, even if it is delivered directly to the desktop, when the problem Sally has is handling angry customers, and John is not able to answer customer questions about how to use the company's Web site? Individual, customized training, geared to address individual customer service agent gaps and weaknesses, is what can lead to improved performance.

The result of the customer service agent skill gaps, is that the people between the company and the customers are inconsistent, inaccurate, inefficient and ineffective at meeting your customers' needs, regardless of how well the call is routed or how accurately customer and company information is popped on the screen. We therefore conclude that delivering individualized refresher training cost-effectively to all customer service agents is crucial to meeting corporate objectives.

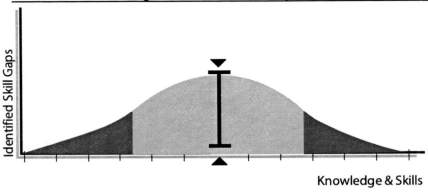

Figure 5.2. Agent performance gaps are individualized

Problem #4: Time

Many times executives will complain, "I want to see butts in seats! Where is everyone?" The perception is that customer service agents aren't delivering value to the organization if they are sitting in a classroom. That's because agents are hired to be on the phones with customers. If they were sitting in a classroom receiving training every time an organization goes through some change, it would be difficult or impossible for an organization to receive the necessary value from these employees. However, at the same time, customer service agents can't deliver value to the organization if they do not have the knowledge and skills to manage customer relationships effectively.

Problem #5: Motivation

The traditional approach to address some of the challenges for improving performance, such as reducing classroom time so that an organization can maintain desired levels of productivity, fail to address the fact that customer service agents are typically dissatisfied with their jobs. The new paradigm for performance is either punitive (de-motivating) or self-directed, not individualized. It's hardly likely that an overworked customer service agent will be motivated to use their downtime to learn new skills. Instead, if training could be proactively pushed to the agent's desktop at the most teachable moment, they might be more interested.

"...as Dell Computer Corporate Vice-president
Theresa Garza puts it, people bring 'hum.' Not the
whirling white noise emanating from your computer,
but the very tangible sense of fully engaged people,
channeling unbound energy into their work. You
know it as soon as you enter a building. It's people
who have momentum, who are working hard, and who
are excited to be there."
—*BusinessWeek*, "The Search for the Young and
Gifted" Oct 4, 1999.

More Best Performers, Faster

Customer service agents have to know the facts, be able to
quickly recall and appropriately package mountains of ever-changing
information in order to meet the company's objectives of increasing
revenue, reducing costs, improving profits, impressing the financial
community and making the shareholders happy. A customer service
agent's performance must improve to meet the new, strategic
expectations of management and participate in the profit growth of
the future. Customer service agents must be able to deliver on the
fundamental mission of the customer service center in a way that is
consistent with the objectives of the business. The mission of the
customer service center is to be the "answer" center—therefore the
customer service agents must have the answers.

Performance can be thought of as the summation of a number of
business objectives met well. Each objective is made up of a series of
metrics that are important to that business objective. The closer we
get to meeting all of the business objectives, the larger is our
company's *wallet share* in the market place.

As we stated earlier, getting agent variability out of the customer
service center is key. With the customer service center representing a
set of repeatable processes—new account activation, change address
or close account—each process can be viewed graphically as
performance by agent as a bell curve (figure 5.3). If 20% of customer
service agents would be significantly below the threshold for the
metric and 20% would be significantly above, naturally, the middle
60% are "in the neighborhood" of the desired threshold.

Decreasing the variability of performance against a given metric
between the middle 60% and the top 20% is what can really move the
needle for a given metric. The bottom 20% consists of new hires and

bad apples. Most of the new hires will move into another category and the bad apples aren't worth saving. You will want to hang on to the top 20% if you can—develop them and hope to keep them in the business. Decreasing the variability of performance in a given metric requires that the behaviors of the middle 60% change to be more like that of the top 20%. Only technology that focuses directly on accelerating time to performance—building more best performers faster, will help companies achieve financial performance.

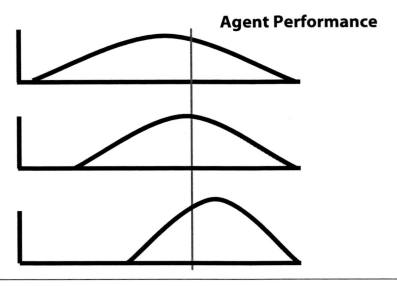

Agent Performance

Figure 5.3. It is important to reduce the variance in customer service agent knowledge.

Putting It All Together

Performance is determined by three components:

1. direction
2. capability
3. motivation

Factors   **Result**

Measurement   ⟶   Direction

Employment   ⟶   Motivation

Training/ Support ⟶ Capability

Outcome ⟶ **More Best Performers**

Figure 5.4. Build best performers

Research has shown that of these three capabilities, training had the most impact on improving performance. Adults generally have a strong preference for learning by "doing." Without learning "what they need to do," they are without direction and are not motivated. In fact, research cited in Harvard Business Review shows that increasing confidence in the ability to handle difficult customers and in responding to the daily questions and requirements contributed significantly to customer service agent job satisfaction and length of employment. Therefore, making sure that the basics are covered— that customer service agents have the knowledge and skills to do their job well—can allow organizations to better leverage and reap a return on investment for these employees.

Learning Theories

If we look back at Edward Thorndike's work (he is noted as one of the greatest learning theorist of all times) the results in the Harvard Business Review article makes sense. Here's why. Thorndike found that behaviors that are followed by pleasant consequences will be more likely to be repeated in the future (Hergenhahn, 1982). So if a customer service agent learns how to deal with a particular problem, and each time they encounter that problem, the result is good, it stands to reason that they will consistently repeat that same solution. The result is that your customers get consistent service. On the other hand, if the customer service agent has no idea how to deal with an issue, and they try something and it does not work, not only do they provide poor service, but they are at a loss for what to do the next time they encounter the same situation. The result? Inconsistent and poor service, leading to caller dissatisfaction.

> ## Training History Fact - Chinese Philosophers
>
> In the 5th-century B.C., the philosopher Lao-Tse (also Lao-tzu) wrote, "If you tell me, I will listen. If you show me, I will see. But if you let me experience, I will learn." And so began one of the first active learning philosophies.
>
> Other Chinese philosophers, such as Kung Fu-tse (Latinized as Confucius) and Han Fei-Tzu, followed Lao-Tse by using a method that closely resembles what we now call the *case method* or *case study*. A member of the study group would present a paradox, which would be in the form of a parable. They would then discuss it and explore possible resolutions.

Malcolm Knowles was one of the first learning researchers to popularize adult learning theory (Leigh, 1999). In his theory he showed that adult learners are driven to change behavior when the information they are being provided is problem-centered and presents solutions to those problems. They gain confidence when they practice what they have learned. Along this line, Discovery Learning, an inquiry based learning method where the person compares the actual experience with the education, is a very effective method of helping employees reach performance goals by learning to think on their feet. One of the earliest references to what Knowles calls discovery learning is the story behind the word EUREKA!

> ## Training History Fact - EUREKA!
>
> Hiero II requested that Archimedes find a method for determining whether a crown was pure gold or alloyed with silver. When the crown was put into water he realized the given weight of gold would displace less water than an equal weight of silver (which is less dense than gold). At this point he shouted, "EUREKA! I have figured it out."

Discovery learning is based on this "Aha!" method. And this is what you want your customer service agents to be saying each time they get it right! Knowles research parallels Jean Piaget's learning theories that show that people cannot be given information which they immediately understand and use (Sleight, 1993). Instead they must build their knowledge through experience with the information.

The experiences allow them to create mental models in their minds so that when a similar situation occurs, they are able to apply the information and be successful. When this has been accomplished, in Piaget's theory, the student has "learned" the information.

Training History Fact – Our Greek Teachers

Aristotle, among the first Greek Philosophers said, "Excellence is an art won by training and practice. We are what we repeatedly do. Excellence, then, is not an act but a habit."

Socrates (470-399 B.C.) engaged his learners by asking questions (known as the Socratic or dialectic method). He often insisted that he really knew nothing, but his questioning skills allowed others to learn by self-generated understanding.

Plato (428-348 B.C.), who was a student of Socrates and the teacher of Aristotle, wrote down the Dialogues, which have inspired thinkers for more than two thousand years. Plato called this process the *dialectic*. It is a question and answer form of arguing with an "expert" on one side and a "searcher" on the other. In the dialogues, the questioning of the expert by the searcher often exposes gaps in the reasoning. It is through this back and forth argument amongst friends (or adversaries) that understanding grows and becomes revealed to the learners. Plato founded what is said to be the first university—his Academy (near Athens) around 385 B.C.

—Don Clark

Adams, in his book, *Motor Learning and Retention*, showed us that if we practice long enough we develop a mental image of what we are doing (Adams, 1977). For example, professional sports players are often known to utter sounds of satisfaction or expletives when they whack the tennis ball because they can instantaneously tell by the feel of the act that it will be successful. Adams says that students must have enough time to develop a complete mental image of the sequence of steps to become proficient in the skill they are attempting to acquire. His research showed that learners without repetition in the real world—while they may have been able to produce a result in the classroom, they were not able to perform it when they returned to work.

Simulations have proven to be effective in the customer service center. Why? Because they are realistic and can be quickly and easily created by subject matter experts with little to no programming experience. By teaching the best practice approach to handling specific recurring customer queries, simulations shorten the time it takes customer service agents to reach proficiency, providing them with the confidence they need to effectively meet critical business objectives.

Training History Fact - Apprenticeship

In the centuries that preceded the introduction of machine-made parts, craftsmanship of a high order was required to manufacture accurate, durable clocks and watches. Such local craft organizations as the Paris Guild of Clockmakers (1544) were organized to control the art of clock making and its apprenticeship. A guild known as the Clockmakers Company, founded in London in 1630, is still in existence. Education for work had its beginning in about 2000 B.C. [organized apprenticeship] for scribes in Egypt. Thus, education for work was organized in such a way that basic knowledge could be developed in a classroom setting and applied skills could be developed on the job.

The rules for governing apprenticeships were included in the Code of Hammurabi, who placed a code of his laws in the temple of Shamash in 2100 B.C. However, apprenticeships did not really become widespread until the Middle Ages. As tools became more complex, and the knowledge and skills to use them became more specialized, parents or others could no longer teach their children everything. Children were apprenticed to craftspersons or artisans who had the specialized skills and tools for a particular trade. In exchange for work, the craftsperson would teach the child the craft at which he was an expert. Apprentices normally lived with the craftsperson, and received no pay except for maintenance, as the learning of a skill was considered highly valuable.

Guilds, associations of people whose interests or pursuits were the same or similar, were an important part in apprenticeship as they established the quality standards for the product and practice. During the peak of the guild system, which occurred between the twelfth and fifteenth centuries, the yeomen were protected by strict regulation of hours, tools, prices, and wages.

—Don Clark

Hull, in his book, *Principles of Behavior*, discovered that when practice periods are spaced apart (distributed practice) performance is superior to learning where practice periods are back to back (massed practice). If learners are allowed to rest or provided some other form of diversion between practice periods, they will reach higher levels of performance than those that do not (Hull, 1943). From this research it makes sense, when training employees, to have training time intermixed with work time. Instead of loading a large course for an agent to pull down at their own convenience, break the content into 10 or 15 minute "learning breaks." To address the continuous learning requirements of customer service agents, learning must be integrated into the daily culture of the customer service center. Instead of requiring agents to disrupt their workflow to attend classes, or depend on the agents to proactively carve out time for learning, integrated approaches with ACD and other call monitoring systems to proactively and consistently deliver short bursts of learning to agents during call downtimes. This will improve retention and incorporate learning into the daily routine of customer service center agents.

Training History Fact - Vestibule Training

In the early 1800s, factory schools were created due to the industrial revolution, in which workers were trained in classrooms within the factory walls. The apprentice system was inadequate due to the number of learners that had to be trained as the machines of the Industrial Revolution increased the ability of the factory to produce goods. The factory owners needed trained workers quickly because there was a large demand for the produced goods.

Towards the end of the 1800s, a method that combined the benefits of the classroom with the benefits of on-the-job training, called vestibule training, became a popular form of training. The classroom was located as close as conditions allowed to the department for which the workers were being trained. It was furnished with the same machines as used in production. There were normally six to ten workers per trainer, who were skilled workers or supervisors from the company.

There are many advantages of vestibule training. The workers are trained as if on the job, but it did not interfere with the more vital task of production. Transfer of skills and knowledge to the workplace was not required since the classroom was a model of the working environment. Classes were small so that the learners received immediate feedback and could ask questions more easily than in a large classroom. Its main disadvantage is that it is quite expensive as it duplicates the production line and has a small learner to trainer ratio.

During World War II, The National Defense Advisory Commission responded to the need for a fast method to train people. They developed a systematic on-the-job training method called JIT (Job Instruction Training). Its goal was to train supervisors in defense plants to train their employees as fast as possible.

—Don Clark

Training History Fact – Motivation to Learn and a System to Training

German philosopher, psychologist, and educator Johann Friedrich Herbart is acknowledged as the "father of scientific pedagogy." Herbart's system of philosophy stems from the analysis of experience. Herbart was the first scientist to distinguish instructional process from subject matter. According to Herbart, interest develops when already strong and vivid ideas are hospitable towards new ones, thus past associations motivate apperception of current ones. **Herbartianism, in predicting that learning follows from building up sequences of ideas important to the individual, gave teachers a semblance of a theory of motivation.**

He also stressed the study of the psychological processes of learning as a means of devising educational programs based on the aptitudes, abilities, and interests of students. The success of Herbart's methods led to their adoption in the teacher-training systems of numerous countries.

Herbart stressed the study of the psychological processes of learning as a means of devising educational programs based on the aptitudes, abilities, and interests of students. The success of Herbart's methods led to their adoption in the teacher-training systems of numerous countries. Based on his work, Herbart's followers designed a five-step teaching method:

1. Prepare the pupils to be ready for the new lesson.

2. Present the new lesson.

3. Associate the new lesson with ideas studied earlier.

4. Use examples to illustrate the lesson's major points.

5. Test pupils to ensure they had learned the new lesson.

— Don Clark

Show, Tell, Do, and Check

Let's look at little closer at the three components of using technology to create more best performers, faster. Our system of direction, capability and motivation, is similar to one developed almost a century ago. To solve an urgent need to train shipyard workers in 1917, Charles R. Allen adapted Herbart's five-step process (Hergenhahn, 1982). He called it the method of job instruction:

- SHOW: Prepare the customer service agents—put at ease. Find out what they already know about the job. Get them interested in learning. Place learning modules in the correct position.

- TELL: Present the operation—tell, show, illustrate, and question carefully and patiently. Stress key points. Instruct clearly and completely, taking up one point at a time, but no more than they can master.

- DO: Try out performance—test them by having them perform the job. Have them tell and show you, have them explain key points. Ask questions and correct answers. Continue until you know that they know.

- CHECK: Follow up—put them on their own. Designate who they go to for help. Check frequently. Encourage questions. Get them to look for key points as they progress. Taper off extra coaching and close follow-ups.

While times have changed a lot, how workers work and what is required to get a job done remains fundamentally the same.

Direction: Tell Me What To Do

Giving employees direction means clearly articulating the goals of the customer service center and then translating those goals into individual tasks expected of the agent. It is important to note that if one customer service agent is answering calls and another is responding to e-mails, the goals for those two different types of jobs may have different performance objectives.

The components of instruction and training with respect to direction are best described by a set of measurable targets, the performance the customer service agents will exhibit when they do the task and the criteria against which their performance will be compared. This last element is important to the third aspect improving performance: motivation: pay me or penalize me. If customer service agents know how they are going to be measured and rewarded, they are more likely to hit the target.

Motivation: Pay Me Or Penalize Me

Motivation and reward are critical components to building best performers, faster. Accenture's CRM study, "What are CRM Capabilities Really Worth?" found that motivating and rewarding people are equally important to improving performance.

Motivation means tell me "What's in it for me?" When customer service agents understand how their individual actions will affect things that matter to them, like pay raise, shift preferences, etc... they can then decide how they want to perform. This requires skillful communication by managers so that the message clearly relates to the things that build best performers (Maslow, 1954). What might motivate a manager or an executive clearly might not motivate a customer service agent. Many times focus groups can be a good source of information for managers to constantly determine if the environment provided in the customer service center is conducive to motivated customer service agents.

Arousal is a major component of motivation. Arousal theories are closely related to other concepts such as anxiety, attention, agitation, stress, and motivation. The arousal level can be thought of as how much capacity you have available to work with. Robert M. Yerkes predicted an inverted U-shaped function between arousal and performance (figure 5.5). A certain amount of arousal can be a motivator toward change (with change in this discussion being learning) (Yerkes, 1908). Too much or too little change will certainly work against the learner. You want some mid-level of arousal to provide the motivation to change (learn). Too little arousal has an inert affect on the learner, while too much has a hyperactive affect. Also, there are optimal levels of arousal for each task to be learned.

Everyone is inspired when they are rewarded. Rewards for customer service agents often come in the form of money or special bonuses, like gift certificates or trips. In Tom Gilberts book, *Human Competence: Engineering Worthy Performance*, he says rewarding accomplishments are the best way to establish repeat behavior. When employees know that they will either be "paid or penalized" based on whether or not they did the job well is the most effective way for organizations to get the greatest pay back on their training and performance improvement investments. This also requires individualization, but this can be easy to implement with technology.

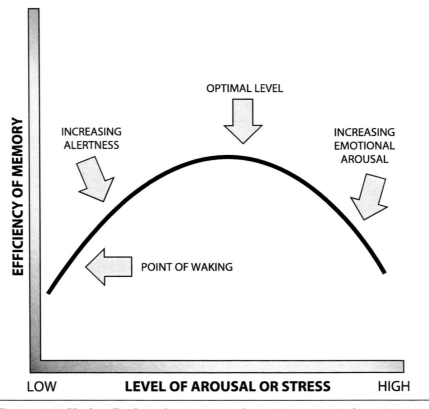

Figure 5.5. Yerkes-Dodson law—arousal requirements in learning

Capability: Show Me How To Do It

Showing customer service agents the myriad of things they need to know is the most difficult to achieve because there is so much information required in order to perform the job properly. It is also difficult because people forget more than 80% of what they learn. It calls for individualization. In addition, the information must be integrated into other customer service center technologies and systems and delivered to take advantage of both forecasted and un-forecasted workflow downtimes.

Performance and Individual Metrics

In order to get customer service agents to perform against individual metrics, there needs to be an overall performance strategy as well as a defined for each metric. Figure 5.6 shows an example of an overall performance strategy.

For a given metric, let's say revenue from cross-sell initiatives, the performance strategy would contain the knowledge components, the required levels of proficiencies and the training method used to achieve proficiency and the motivation incentive. Figure 5.7 shows an example of a learning strategy for a particular metric.

Once the performance strategy for each metric is determined, then the knowledge and skill gaps must be identified as it relates to a metric. Each knowledge and skill gap would then have an associated learning module to help the customer service agent close the gap.

What Can You Do?

A Performance Strategy is a plan for lifting and sustaining agent performance.

Performance Strategy	INTERACTIVE PLANNING		
		Individual Agents	Supervisors/Mgrs.
Learning Plan	Discovery	• Identify individual knowledge and skill gaps within an agent population	
	Opportunity	• Align employee performance with company objectives • Drive employee effectiveness	
	Technique	• Simulation, coaching, interactive gaming, recurrent and frequent training delivery	
	Timing	• The most teachable moment • Deliver training during downtimes in call volume	
	Validation	• Results • Success? Failure? To what extent?	

Figure 5.6. A performance strategy is necessary to accomplish the business goals and objectives of the business and therefore, the customer service center.

Knowledge Components	Proficiency	Training Method
Sales Basics		Multimedia courses, examples
Qualifying the Customer		Exercises, quizzes
Handling Objections		Games, simulations
Closing Questions		Best practices, scenarios

Figure 5.7. For a given metric, revenue from cross-sell initiatives, the performance strategy is composed of the knowledge components, proficiency and training methods.

> "...for thousands of years, humans have been discussing the meaning of knowledge, what it is to know something, and how people can generate and share new knowledge."
> — *Knowledge Management Tools*,
> Rudy L. Ruggles, III, 1997

What if We Close the Gap?

Why does changing agent performance matter? By changing how we give customer service agents direction, capability and motivation, the performance of customer service agents change. And when performance is improved—efficiency and effectiveness show up in the bottom-line, figure 5.8.

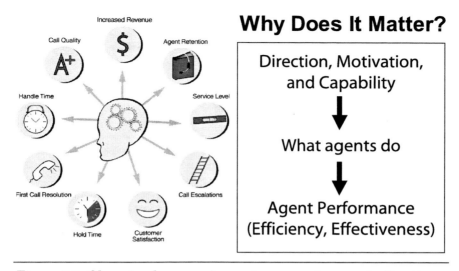

Why Does It Matter?

Direction, Motivation, and Capability

↓

What agents do

↓

Agent Performance (Efficiency, Effectiveness)

Figure 5.8. Changing how we give customer service agents direction, motivation, learning and incentives shows up on our bottom-line.

Let's look at some statistics and how they relate to the bottom-line. We can see bottom-line affects from things like

- average handle time,
- customer service agent turnover,
- quality of customer interaction, and
- cross selling skills & product knowledge.

Here's why average handle time (AHT) impacts staffing budgets. Customer service agent turnover impacts operating costs. Cross selling skills and product knowledge impacts revenue and the quality of customer interaction affects customer loyalty and long term revenue and profit growth. Let's look at each of these individually, assuming a 1,000-seat customer service center.

Here's how AHT impacts staffing budgets. If it costs $12/hour per customer service agent, or $24,000/year, then a 5% reduction in AHT essentially reduces staffing requirements by 5%. In a 1,000 seat center, the annual savings is $1,200,000.

Industry average "cost" of hiring a new customer service agent is $8,000. If a 1,000-seat customer service center has an annual turnover of 40%, a 10% improvement results in annual savings of $320,000.

If customer service agents handle 150 inbound calls per day and if 5% of those transactions are not satisfying the customer, that results in 1,875,000 bad customer experiences per year. If the revenue of each customer is $25, and they decide not to buy again, the lost revenue is ~$46 million dollars.

If a customer service agent's daily gross sales revenue is $4,000, a 5% increase (or decrease) in gross sales per customer service agent results in $50,000,000 annual impact.

What Can We DO?

In order to sustain the maximum level of customer service, companies must clarify and prioritize their critical business objectives, identify key performance objectives that can be directly linked to financial gain, then develop a closed-loop strategy for building more best performers, faster. Your company will benefit in the form of increased revenue, improved productivity, a higher level of customer satisfaction or simply reduced operating costs.

Ultimately, improved agent performance can be measured through an overall improvement in your organization's bottom line. By focusing on creating an effective rather than efficient team of best performers, you'll see not only immediate rewards, but also continued and accelerated growth as knowledge levels deepen and turnover rates subside. You'll be steering an organization built on the strongest foundation of all—good, knowledgeable and motivated people.

The Goal: Best Performers, Faster

As companies are continuously challenged not only to deliver more sophisticated sales and service capabilities, but also to manage these capabilities more quickly and cost effectively, executives will eventually conclude that the only way to compete effectively is to fill customer service centers with more best performers—faster. And that capability causes a profound needle move.

The way to a customer's heart lies not in software, systems and processes, but in people. In Chapter 5, it became very apparent that in order for the company to attain its goals, the customer service center has to have a way to address the individualized agent knowledge and skill gaps. While organizations have made considerable expenditures to deliver calls smarter and faster to customer service agents, and to retroactively monitor performance with quality monitoring systems, only a fraction of investment is made to proactively ensure consistently well-trained agents are prepared to effectively handle customer calls. As a result, many organizations are simply delivering bad service to their customers faster, and investing inordinate amounts of expensive time coaching their worst customer service agents after the damage is already done to the customer relationship. This is sometimes referred to as "automating the mess."

Performance In the Customer Service Center: Is It Broken?

Remember when we were in grade school or even in junior high? Most of us took the same curriculum—we all needed the basics of reading, writing and arithmetic. The teacher presented the materials in a group lecture and study format, which seemed appropriate because we each needed to learn the same things and we were developing new knowledge at the same time. Initial training in the customer service center is handled a lot like this because everyone is learning a new "subject" together. And often times, when we do succeed in getting customer service agents into training after the new hire orientation, we ignore the individual's knowledge needs. Yet, there is constantly so much new information the customer service agent needs to know. Imagine being invited to a restaurant that delivered the same food to everyone, regardless of what they ordered:

Customer: "I'll have the lamb chops."
Server: "Enjoy the pizza."
Or
Customer: "I'll have the fillet."
Server: "Enjoy the pizza."

This is what we do in the customer service centers when it comes to on-going training. The "holes" in the knowledge will naturally occur as we've discussed. Like an old boat that needs to be plugged, holes will continue to appear in each agent's knowledge. We know the human brain will continually forget. Although reinforcement will make knowledge stickier, new information and change is inevitable in the customer service center. Therefore, on-going training MUST be done, and we must be able to deliver it on an individual-by-individual basis.

One solution is this: change the teacher to student ratio. Customer service centers could dramatically lower their customer service agent-to-trainer ratio (from 150-to-1 to around 3-to-1) by hiring significantly more trainers (obviously not a likely scenario). Through our benchmark research, we have found that

- initial training averages 15 days,
- ongoing training averages < 2 hours/month,
- 84% train exclusively in the classroom despite advances in training technology and relative inefficiencies of the classroom,
- one trainer for every 121 employees is normal, and
- no regular measurement of training ROI exists.

In figure 6.1 we see how training is often done today without technology. Many of the issues we talked about in the previous chapters come to light as we review this list. However, what we will find out in this chapter is that these issues can be solved with technology if it provides an integrated e-learning solution.

Initial Training

- Small groups
- Instructor-lead
- Mostly systems, policies, and product
- Hands-on, but fault tolerant
- A lot of coaching
- We're doing this the right way!
- We're not measuring, however.

Ongoing Training

- Delivered to large groups
- Usually policies and product
- Frequent
- Not hands-on, not fault tolerant
- Little coaching
- Delivered with no concern for workflows
- We're doing this the wrong way!

Figure 6.1. Most training today is broken

Learning Styles

Individual learning styles have a lot to do with retention. David Kolb's *Experiential Learning: Experience As the Source of Learning and Development* (Kolb, 1984) theorized that people develop preferences for different learning styles in the same way that they develop any other sort of style, i.e., management, leadership, negotiating, etc. To understand the value of the learning inventory, learners must first have a basic understanding of the experiential learning model and know what their preferred learning style is. This model provides a framework for identifying students' learning style preferences (figure 6.2).

Kolb found that the four combinations of perceiving and processing determine the four learning styles. According to Kolb, the learning cycle involves four processes that must be present for learning to occur:

- **Activist**—Active experimentation (simulations, case study, homework). What's new? I'm game for anything. Here the training approach is problem solving, small group discussions, peer feedback, and homework. A trainer should allow the learner to determine her own criteria for relevance of materials.

- **Reflector**—Reflective observation (logs, journals, brainstorming). I'd like time to think about this. Here the training approach is lectures. A trainer should provide expert interpretation (taskmaster/guide) and judge performance by external criteria.

- **Theorist**—Abstract conceptualization (lecture, papers, analogies). How does this relate to that? Here the training approach is via case studies, theory readings and self-reflection. Almost everything else, including talking with experts, is not helpful.

- **Pragmatist**—Concrete experience (laboratories, field work, observations). How can I apply this in practice? Here the training approach is via peer feedback. Activities should apply skills where the trainer is coach/helper for the self-directed autonomous learner.

Kolb's Experiential Learning Style

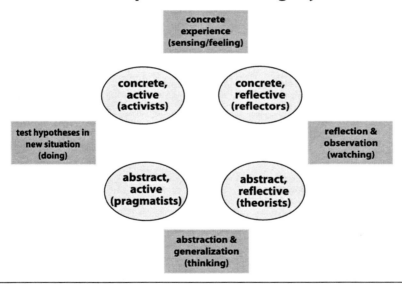

Figure 6.2. Kolb theorized that people develop preferences for different learning styles.

The differences in learning styles can challenge trainers when developing training. Most of our educational systems assume that learners can learn the same information in the same way. While e-learning technology may not be able to provide the exact learning style to each and every individual, it does increase the odds of success because it provides multiple formats for the material. Knowledge transfer and skill assessment training for customer service agents can consists of both knowledge transfer elements (classroom type lecture) and skill assessment elements (role play calls, practice calls, etc.). When we realize that all learning is social, i.e., people learn by talking with others and finding out what worked for them in informal conversations, we can see how e-learning gives the learner the freedom to learn this way (rather than cramming their brains with repetitive exercises and exams).

> "Learning strengthens the brain. In other words, the more you learn, the more capable you are of learning. While children learn by building new pathways, adult brains make new arrangements of existing sequences by building new neural pathways."
> —Marcia Conner of Learnativity

From a neurological aspect, established knowledge from experience and background is made up of exceedingly intricate arrangements of cell materials, electrical charges and chemical elements. "This is why learning requires energy and why re-learning requires even more energy. In re-learning we must access higher brain functions to create the energy to unbind the old information," says Conner (Conner, 2000).

Chocolate Chip Cookies and Performance

 So what does the smell of fresh baked cookies or bread have to do with performance? Everything. Neurologists have shown the sense of smell, the olfactory sense, is the strongest and longest retained in memory. The reason for this is because smell is a sensory memory that readily associates itself with all others. When you remember a favorite place, event or person, it is often the scent of food, perfume or something that calls up that memory. We learn best by engaging as many senses as possible. This is the reason why apprenticeships were so successful. Remember the story of the apprentice in Chapter 5? Apprentices learned their trade so quickly because there was full sensory interaction (hands-on learning), one-to-one tutelage and the time and materials to practice what they would be doing on the job. With full-sensory involvement, more neural pathways are engaged and result in more associative bonds between established ones (Conner, 2000; Kolb, 1989). The apprenticeship training method allowed a learner to be exposed to a learning style that best suited them because all learning modalities were included.

The Institute for Learning Styles Research identifies at least seven perceptual learning styles. A perceptual learning style is defined as the means by which learners extract information from their surroundings using their senses. Two senses (visual and tactile) are involved in more than one of the total seven. When information, enters a pathway that is best suited for that person, it is retained in the short-term memory. Repeated exposure and use promote long-term memory. The seven perceptual modes or pathways include:

- **Print**—seeing the printed word
- **Aural**—listening to information
- **Interactive**—verbalizing the information
- **Visual**—seeing pictures and graphs
- **Haptic**—touching it
- **Kinesthetic**—the body moving
- **Olfactory**—smelling and tasting

When G. Millbank, in *Writing Multi-media Training with Integrated Simulation*, studied mixing audio with video in a corporate training versus without either, the retention rate of the students jumped from 20% to 75% (Millbank, 1994). What is important to remember is that learners learn in many different modes and the training should try to provide as many as possible.

Corporate Politics versus Customer Service Center Performance Initiatives

The job of a customer service agent is unlike that of anyone else in the company. In that way, the customer service center is like an island, a company within a company. Sure, every job in a company is different. BUT the job of a customer service agent is vastly different than any other employee—it is another world. If you combine the job of a blind bank teller at a busy bank and that of the person manning the information desk at Boston's Logan airport (a city that is vast and always under construction), you'll start to get the picture. The customer service agent has no control over their workflow. They have to deal with queues they can't see. And they must efficiently deal accurate information to customers drawing from a mountain of ever-changing information. How is it this job, that is not even remotely similar to anything else in the corporation, is treated the same from a training perspective? The training requirements are so much more intensive and job-critical, that the training must be treated differently.

In our research and consulting we have interacted with thousands of corporate trainers at hundreds of large corporations. Less than 10% of these people understand the job of the customer service agent. Most often, the ones who did understand the job had actually been customer service agents themselves. By and large, corporate trainers do not have an authentic understanding of the unique performance requirements of the customer service center—and this is a problem. Everyone knows what a customer service center's function is and since the rest of the organization is duly served by the corporate training organization, it is easy to conclude that the customer service center could be also.

Where this issue gets sticky is that corporate training organizations generally do training for all employees. They are paid to know the training needs of the company. The most common response of this group is a defensive one, saying (essentially), "I am the training expert and you are the customer service center expert. I know what is best for you." Imagine how you would feel if the VP of Training came to you to get your support for a technology to route calls! Compounding the problem, however, is that corporate training is an organization that does not enjoy a great deal of power in the organization. When management approaches the training organization with the special training needs of the customer service center they feel like it is another coup and loss of power. If there is an organization that gets less respect than the customer service center, it is probably corporate training.

So the question is what can you do about it?

One approach is to attempt to gain their agreement. Using this approach, you could help the corporate training organization understand your unique challenges. You could explain the way in which your business operates. This is the high road. Unfortunately, it has been the experience of many that it is the long road—one which many customer service center executives do not have the patience and time for.

Another option is to go your own way. Many frustrated customer service center executives have thrown up their hands and forced a solution on the training group using their own budgets. While faster, this is a higher risk course because the corporate training group did not bless the solution.

CBT Versus an Integrated Strategy

Another solution many companies consider is computer-based training or CBT (Saettler, 1968) (Gagne, 1987) (Ruttenbur, 2000). However, like corporate training, traditional CBT learning tools are not designed for the unique needs of the customer service center (Adria, 2002). Traditional CBT tools are primarily about *availability* and *self-directed learning*. In sharp contrast, the customer service center learning environment requires the *delivery* of *individualized* (selected) learning.

Remember your first day on campus at college? Did the Dean of Students walk up to you in to the middle of campus, point out the library and say, "In that building are 160,000 books. Everything that you will need to learn is in that building. In four years, you will take a test and get your degree." This is analogous to traditional CBT systems, i.e., availability and self-direction. But that kind of system doesn't really work for customer service centers.

What does work is more like the courses offered by the school to fill the gaps that existed in our individualized degree program. In that scenario, every quarter we attended classes to increase our knowledge. This format is much like the needs of the customer service center—it supports the delivery of individualized learning.

Canned Versus Customized

Another choice you might be faced with is looking at canned versus customized training. If you remember that the customer service agent's job is company-specific, i.e., the job of a customer service center is to provide support to customers and potential customers on a company's products and services, then you can begin to see how canned products just don't fit the bill. In addition, customer service agents utilize software systems to do their job that are, at best, custom installations of software products, if not all together homegrown systems. So the priority for custom training on company products, pricing, promotions, policies, procedures and systems usually takes priority over canned training on things like soft skills. Canned training (usually on soft skills) is important, but is unfortunately not viewed important by customer service center executives who are responsible for delivering the metrics that impact the bottom line.

An Integrated Solution

What we have learned to this point is that customer service centers have more interaction with customers than any other part of the business. Customer service agents are on the front line and greatly influence the customer's perception of the company. We also know that increased learning provides "Job Enrichment" ... a key factor for job satisfaction (i.e., reduced staff turnover) (Shea-Shultz, 2002). And since there is a direct correlation between staff turnover and customer churn, as well as a direct correlation between improved service quality and reduced customer churn, the issue of how to best train customer service agents needs an out-of-the-box solution, now!

What executives need is an effective performance optimization program that will improve quality and customer satisfaction while reducing both staff and customer churn. One approach to ensure **focus on customer success** is to use a *prioritized*, *systematic*, *data driven* approach, which can bring rapid and profound benefits to customers. In this type of performance model it must be able execute the learning strategy with:

- easy authoring of multiple content types
- simulation authoring of the customer service center environment
- delivery without loss of productivity
- data-driven targeted training to ensure content is prioritized and helpful
- validation to motivate customer service agents and validate purpose
- sustainable knowledge/skill building
- management and monitoring of scores, times taken, across audiences and customer service centers

If we use a balanced score card approach there are four key measurement areas:

1. financial
2. customer satisfaction
3. internal processes
4. learning and development

Underlying the theory of the balanced score card is the fact that learning and growth pushes results in all other areas of the business.

So how can we facilitate increased learning? The process begins with understanding the performance gap. The next step is to develop a learning strategy to close the gap. Software that can aggressively close the gap *and* sustain a high level of performance is required. The last step is a way to prove bottom-line success to the board of directors and top executives.

Ideal Components of an Integrated System for Customer Service Centers

So what are the ideal components of an integrated performance optimization system? Remember back in Chapter 5 we looked at the five main obstacles preventing performance improvement? Those included the fact that performance improvement is

- in conflict with operational goals,
- customer service agents forget what they learn,
- skills gaps are individualized,
- there's no time to do the training, and
- the customer service agents aren't motivated to learn.

We also realized that there is a gap between the employee's objectives and the business objectives (figure 6.3). And often times if there is a performance strategy, like the one in figure 6.4, it is difficult to determine where the gaps are and how to solve them (figure 6.5). What is required is a performance system that is integrated with all the other customer service center technologies so that the performance management system can deliver the right content at the right time (figure 6.6).

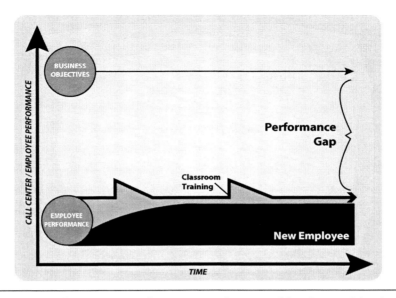

Figure 6.3. There is a gap between employee and business objectives.

What Can You Do?

A Performance Strategy is a plan for lifting and sustaining agent performance.

Performance Strategy	INTERACTIVE PLANNING	
	Individual Agents	**Supervisors/Mgrs.**
Discovery	• Identify individual knowledge and skill gaps within an agent population	
Opportunity	• Align employee performance with company objectives • Drive employee effectiveness	
Technique	• Simulation, coaching, interactive gaming, recurrent and frequent training delivery	
Timing	• *The most teachable moment* • Deliver training during downtimes in call volume	
Validation	• Results • Success? Failure? To what extent?	

Figure 6.4. A performance strategy helps to fill the gap between employees and business objectives.

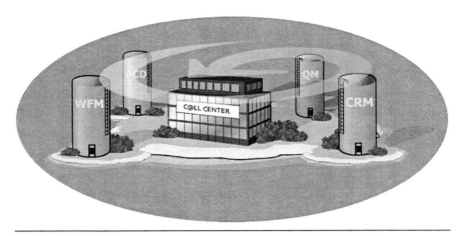

Figure 6.5. It can be difficult to determine where the gap in performance lies because there are so many variables between work force management (WFM), customer relationship management (CRM), automatic call distributor (ACD) and quality management (QM).

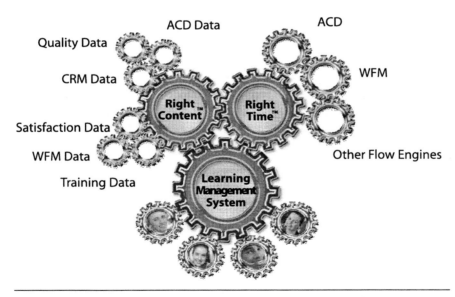

Figure 6.6. Deliver the right content at the right time with an integrated agent performance management solution

Training Content

To resolve the issues we have been grappling with throughout this book, the ideal components for customer service center learning systems should first enable and support

1. development of effective learning content,
2. management of course content,
3. creation of learning development plans,
4. integration delivery platforms, and
5. evaluation of self-paced training courses for customer service agents.

Courses need to be designed to reinforce on-going quality assurance coaching, assist in the launch of new products and programs, and increase the overall knowledge of the customer service agents. Figure 6.7 shows an example of an individual's proficiencies versus a benchmarked best practice. In addition, the e-learning system should be used as part of the new-hire training program. The goal is to provide effective efficiency by the agents accomplishing assigned tasks correctly and completely with a minimum of resources. Agent performance can then be defined as *effective efficiency in line with company objectives* (figure 6.8).

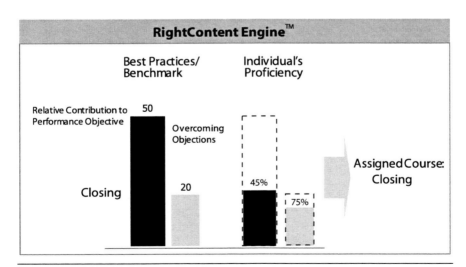

Figure 6.7. When best practices are compared to the individual proficiencies, via a performance system, the courses required to help a customer service agent become proficient can be assigned.

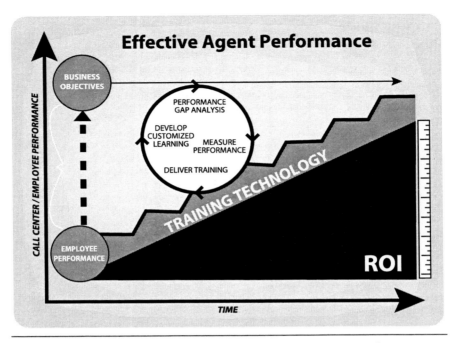

Figure 6.8. Agent's performance is aligned with business objectives

Administration Tools

An integrated agent performance management system requires administration tools allowing managers to assign specific courses to individual customer service agents to address their individual performance gaps and skill deficiencies (figures 6.9 and 6.10). In addition, it is necessary to schedule individual customer service agent training sessions during forecasted periods of low call volume, when agents are likely to have down time (figure 6.11). Managers will want to track training activity and progress at the following levels:

- enterprise
- customer service center
- team
- individual agent

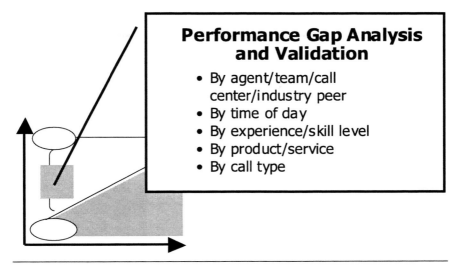

Figure 6.9. Individual performance gaps and skill deficiencies are identified

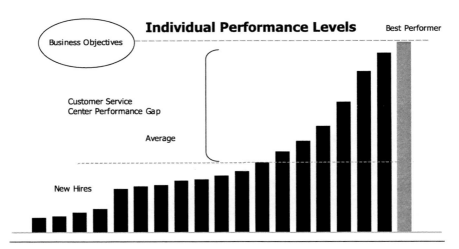

Figure 6.10. Individual performance gaps and skill deficiencies are targeted in the training to reduce the customer service center performance gap

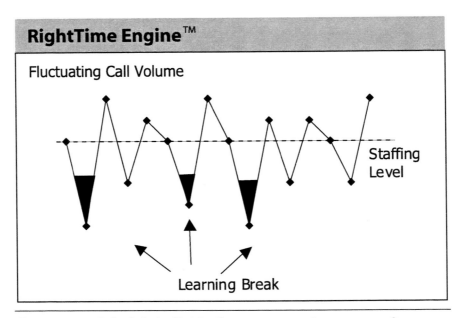

Figure 6.11. Schedule individual customer service agent performance improvement sessions during forecasted periods of low call volume

It is important that the agent performance system is able to integrate with other customer service center systems to support the scheduling and delivery of training, including the

- automatic call distributor (ACD),
- workforce management system, and
- call recording and quality monitoring systems.

When the training system is integrated with the ACD (figure 6.6), unforecasted slow times can be can identified for when unscheduled training breaks can occur (figure 6.11). It should also be able to alert customer service agents currently taking a course to suspend training and return to the phones when the number of calls waiting exceeds a certain threshold. In addition, it should be able to deliver simulated calls via computer telephony integration (CTI) to customer service agents when they are using the course. It is important to have the training system integrated with the workforce management system (figure 6.6), to download scheduled training breaks to ensure that learning is completed at times which minimize or avoid a negative impact to customer service levels.

The role of the call recording and quality monitoring system should be able to identify individual skill gaps and determine which courses to assign to individual customer service agents to fix their skill gaps (figure 6.7). It is important that the system be able to monitor the customer service agents interaction with various desktop applications and identify areas where the agent could be more efficient in migrating through the system and more effective in interpreting the data in the system (figure 6.9). In addition, it is important to be able to determine applicable courses and/or call simulations to assign to individual agents to address the efficiency and effectiveness gaps identified (figure 6.10).

Delivery Time of Training

The system should contain integrated modules that enable computer-based, online curriculum to be accessed by customer service agents from their desktops during times of reduced customer calls (figure 6.11). These courses might also be presented to customer service agents in a classroom environment to augment and reinforce on-going training in new products, product upgrades, as well as for screen navigation training. Typically, an integrated performance solution is implemented on computer hardware systems that already reside within the customer service center network.

Authoring Tools

An integrated performance solution generally includes authoring tools to support an adult learning model (figure 6.12), in the creation of

- learning modules,
- "real world" simulations,
- tests and quizzes, and
- reference libraries and knowledge bases.

Learning modules allow course developers to leverage existing documents, format text, insert graphics, add gaming and interactivity, as well as incorporate audio and video content. "Real world" simulations of customer calls replicate both the screen navigation and the verbal interaction with the customer via the phone system. Tests and quizzes are incorporated to measure knowledge retention and skill proficiency. Reference libraries and knowledge bases for courses, assessments, call simulations, and interactive games, allow customer service agents to easily access specific content modules at the point of need. And with what we learned about the importance of how the different learning styles impact training retention, you can see how important intuitive authoring tools are to the success of the whole training program.

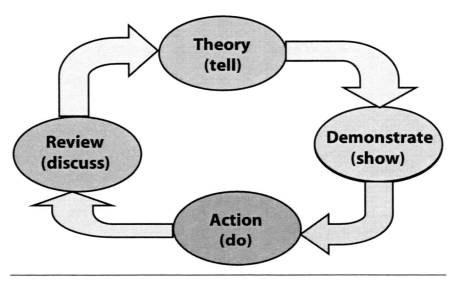

Figure 6.12. The adult learning model

Customer Service Agent Performance Portal

Training systems that have an agent performance portal are more effective. This is because the customer service agent performance portal becomes the interface that provides access for the agent to take courses and experience call simulations. In addition, this is where the customer service agent should be able to find

- updated information about products, promotions, and programs,
- policies and system changes the customer service agent needs to be aware of in order to perform his/her job effectively,
- center-wide announcements, daily refresher questions, quizzes and courseware to reinforce training and ensure knowledge retention, and
- current learning statistics including: listings of assigned courses, review scores and scheduled training breaks.

Call Simulations

You will also want your training system to have a call simulator that allows the customer service agent to interact with a pre-recorded customer voice through their telephone headset, as well as to capture and assess the customer service agent's dialog and screen navigation interaction. This will allow you to provide immediate online coaching, feedback and assistance to the customer service agent. In addition, they should be able to play back simulated calls and screen interactions to coaches and supervisors to allow the evaluation of the agent's performance at a later time.

Reporting and Analytic Tools

In order to track individual customer service agent progress through each assigned course you will need reporting and analytic tools. In addition, you will need to be able to use analytics to determine the effectiveness of each course as well as the agent's retention of the course material. If you have reporting that shows which modules are most commonly studied, which groups have which skills gaps and level of improvement, you will have a better handle on what is working and what is not and where to make changes and improvements. In most training situations the trainers have no real way to determine if what they have designed works or not.

Learning and Development Tools

When your key business objectives have been identified, a team of expert learning strategists can design a customized learning environment that aligns employee objectives with those objectives that ultimately drive revenue for your company. To identify key business objectives that the customer service center can support, you will need a learning and development tool like the one in figure 6.13 that helps to identify

- key business objectives the customer service center supports,
- what, with regard to customer service agent performance, is impeding the achievement of the identified business objective(s),
- target courses, call simulations and review questions necessary to close the identified skill gaps at the customer service center, team, and customer service agent levels, and

- appropriate audience, frequency, and timing of assessments necessary to evaluate the effectiveness of each learning activity.

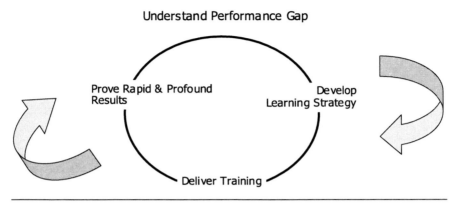

Figure 6.13. The process of delivering service that exceeds business goals

In summary, with a methodology to systematically deliver a process to model, predict, deliver, and prove rapid and profound business results (figure 6.14), you will be able to increase the customer capabilities we discussed in Chapter 1. Furthermore, from the results of the Accenture and AT&T studies, you can begin to see how this could all lead you to increase sales, and therefore profit growth.

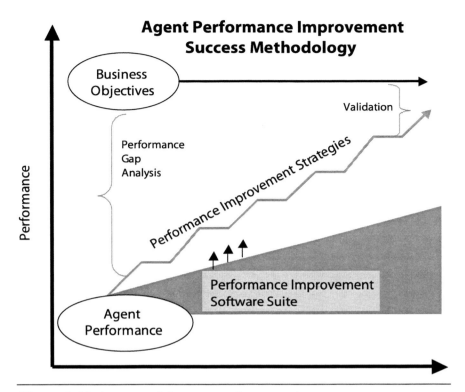

Figure 6.14. A successful agent performance improvement methodology

With a performance strategy you will have a roadmap for closing the performance gaps. You can use a data and research driven series of learning plans to apply the right content and learning technique, at the most effective moment, or "just in time learning." And with a learning software suite tailored to your e-learning platform, it will support authoring, scheduling, delivering, monitoring, and reporting the right training to the person at just the right time. Once the system is in place, the best practice example calls, for each skill group, can be sent to all customer service agents as part of the on-going learning program. In addition, the system may be able to build a skills matrix of people that can input into skills-based routing data on incoming calls. If you deploy a system like this, you will be able to improve agent performance more quickly, more predictably, and more profoundly than with any other alternative.

Examples of How It Can Work

Here are a few examples of how an integrated e-learning system was able to produce significant financial gain for its customers. Figure 6.15 is an example of how a learning strategy to improve sales close ratios can be designed and implemented. Here the *content strategy* is to provide the top five best practices for closing sales, which include

1.   assumptive closes,
2.   alternative closes,
3.   standing room only closes,
4.   last-chance closes, and
5.   order blank closes.

Techniques for building best performers might include

- simulation,
- gaming,
- interactive courses,
- classroom,
- dynamic quizzing,
- bulletin board/tip of the day, and
- coaching.

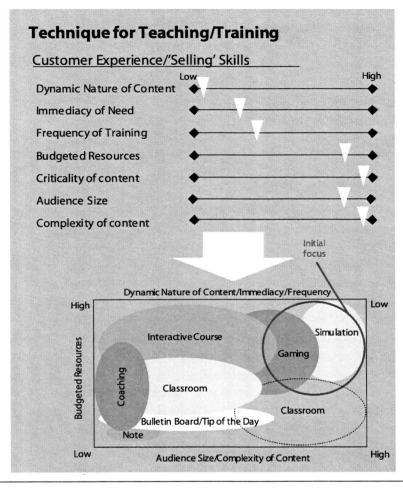

Figure 6.15. An example of how a performance strategy can improve sales closing ratios

The timing strategy could be as follows:

- **Forecast downtimes**:
  Mondays, Wednesdays, Fridays
- **Unforecast downtimes**:
  0 in queue, >15% of reps available
- **Duration**:
  <15 minutes/customer service agent/training day
- **Right to refuse?**:
  No.

AT&T Broadband

Here's how it worked for one customer service center. AT&T Broadband, also known as "a large cable provider," needed help. They realized that service levels at AT&T Broadband were very poor. Even if the company were to add 100 additional customer service agents, service levels would remain poor. They wanted to see if an integrated e-learning system could help them stop losing money.

AT&T was experiencing problems with unnecessary truck dispatches. When a customer called in with an issue—such as static on his television set—the customer service agent would almost always send a service truck to the customer site. The company realized that many of these truck dispatches could have been avoided if the customer service agent had asked some basic troubleshooting and diagnostic questions. In many cases, the customer's problem stemmed from something as simple as a loose cable.

By using an integrated e-learning system, AT&T Broadband developed a learning strategy that taught customer service agents how to troubleshoot most basic problems over the phone before sending a service truck to the customer site. Unnecessary truck dispatches decreased from 11,685 to 6,523 in the first four months. At $70 per dispatched truck, this saved the company some $361,340 per month.

CitiFinancial

CitiFinancial, formerly Associates Capital Bank, required customer service agents to sell 54 different financial products and services to customers. Because of the heavy knowledge burden, most customer service agents stuck to selling the three to four products with which they were the most familiar. An integrated agent performance solution pinpointed which products and services customer service agents needed more information about in order to cross-sell and up-sell to customers and designed a series of courses that encouraged them to offer customers at least one additional product during every call.

CitiFinancial was able to double monthly sales after implementing the integrated performance solution platform. Monthly sales doubled from $2.4 million to more than $4.4 million in the first six months.

The Performance Chain

Although we often view the term *technology* as hardware items, its origination was from the Greeks, and it started with a much different meaning. To the Greeks it was a system of practical knowledge. Technology, derived from the ancient Greek word "techne," means art, craft or skill. Plato viewed "techne" and systematic or scientific knowledge as being closely related. Aristotle went a step further by asserting that "techne" was the systematic use of knowledge for intelligent human action (Hergenhahn, 1982). Perhaps Plato and Aristotle were the frontrunners of what we term today, performance management.

Performance management is a powerful and systematic approach to forging a competitive advantage. It is a blueprint for translating an organization's goals into the objectives and initiatives that drive performance. The reason a performance management system is so critical to an organization, is that it provides

- strategic focus,
- objectives,
- alignment and process,
- indicators,
- monitoring, and
- improvement.

Organizations need a systematic way to grow, develop, and improve. Figure 7.1 provides an example of a road map for a performance management system. Each company has its own needs and generally creates a customized version of this to suit their business model. Here we go over some of the main components and how they can be applied to the customer service center to assure that the goal of profit growth we looked at in Chapter 1 is obtained.

A system of performance management is crucial to quality leadership because it provides management with a systematic way of evaluating human performance. As we learned in Chapter 4, quality needs to be built in, not inspected in. In manufacturing, the integration of quality in manufacturing came in the form of greater emphasis on, and expectations from, human performance. This is also the case in the customer service center. We can now see that customer service agent performance cannot be dealt with punitively—after the "product" or the call has been manufactured. Executives need an effective performance program that will improve quality and caller satisfaction while reducing both staff turnover, and customer churn.

In Chapter 5 we learned that the facilities, technology, processes and measurements in the customer service center have all evolved over time. However, consistency, accuracy, efficiency and effectiveness continue to be a problem. Again, these are all agent performance issues. Customer service agents wind up being the weak link in the customer service center. To perform to our highest expectations, customer service agents must provide accurate information efficiently, and politely. They must have the tools they need to persuade customers to buy more products. Companies need a way to measure their customer service agents' performance and their level of success to determine exactly what needs to be changed.

In order to accomplish these new aspects of the customer service center, agents need to perform more quickly and more predictably. For example, if an agent's knowledge improves, then they can respond more quickly to customer needs and service level, hold time and handle time improve. So if the customer service agent's knowledge and skills are the drivers of every critical metric in the customer service center, that means managers need performance management strategy to guide this. This strategy must be designed to improve performance to achieve the key business objectives.

We learned in Chapter 6 that one approach to ensure focus on customer success is to use a prioritized, systematic, data driven approach, which can bring rapid and profound benefits to customers. The performance of each customer service agent, namely, how well they can handle thousands of customer contacts is important because it affects revenue. The way that a customer service agent's performance affects revenue is in how they handle a sale or build a relationship with a customer that leads to customer loyalty and therefore more sales. By aligning the mission of the customer service center with corporate objectives, it will allow executives to more effectively meet their strategic and financial goals.

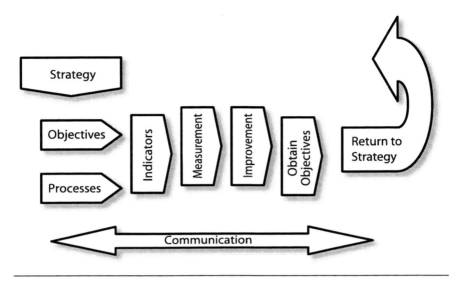

Figure 7.1. A performance chain in the management process

Strategic Focus

The first step in performance management is to determine the strategic focus by evaluating the following:

- where the organization is today
- where the organization wants to be
- how it's going to get there

This information enables the identification of the key areas in which the organization must succeed and helps to create a set of realistic and complementary objectives to produce success. Without this focus, you can waste effort and resources on work that will bring only marginal improvement. Part of this process is to determine the critical success factors. These are the do-or-die aspects of an organization's objectives. The entire success of the organization depends on these factors. You may also want to do a SWOT analysis of your organization (Kouzes, 1995). This is a simple analytical technique that focuses on the positive and negative factors that impact an organization internally and externally. SWOT stands for **S**trengths, **W**eaknesses, **T**hreats, and **O**pportunities.

Objectives

Objectives specify how your business strategy is to be achieved. Objectives translate your strategy statements into quantifiable targets. For example, the vision, *to be the leading supplier of golf products in the United States,* could be defined as capturing a 40% share of the United States golf product market within the next five years.

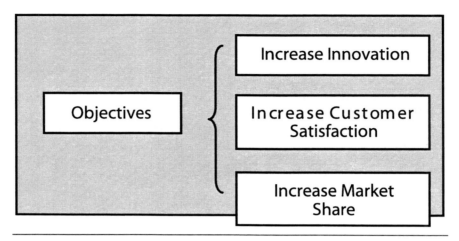

Figure 7.2. Objectives come from the strategy

Objectives are the core from which your organization can define the behaviors that will enable it to achieve its aims. They identify the measures that your organization will use to track its progress, and help identify the initiatives that will improve your performance. For example, to capture a 40% market share, an organization could innovate products, implement initiatives to raise customer service, and set targets for the number of sales leads and closes. Objectives should

- cover the medium to long term,
- contribute to the organization's performance,
- be realistic,
- be agreed, owned, and visible, and
- not be purely financially oriented.

Important here is to consider the difference between MBO (management by objective) and MBP (management by process). Figure 7.3 shows the difference in the two approaches. MBO is used in management by results type leadership and MBP is used in quality leadership that we spoke about in Chapter 4 (Petouhoff and Koons, 2003).

Management By Objective	Management By Process
Control *by* the end results	Control *over* the process to obtain the objectives
More concerned about the results	More concerned about the in-process plan and procedures
Focus on motivation - how to establish goals and improve one's job	Focus on cooperation and coordination - how to establish goals and an organization-wide plan at all levels
More emphasis on how to improve each individual	More emphasis on how to strengthen the process to strengthen the individual
To accomplish the goal, individuals are proceeding with their own plan and ideas	To accomplish the goal, every department is focused on systematic cooperation

Figure 7.3. Management by process is preferred to build in quality

Managers will want to do an initial operational review to get an objective snapshot of the customer service center environment (figure 7.4). The goal of analysis of the center is to:

1. identify overriding business objectives of your organization

2. identify hindrances and inefficiencies preventing your organization from meeting these objectives

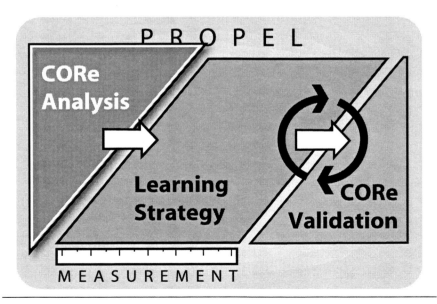

Figure 7.4. Three steps to obtaining results

You might consider bringing in a team of experts to help with the review and analysis. Remember in Chapter 4, when we looked at the idea of innovation. Joel Barker was quoted as saying, "The power of paradigms is that they physiologically affect our ability to see the world. Quite literally, what is obvious to one person may be totally invisible to another. The most likely person to change a paradigm is an OUTSIDER, someone who does not know or practice the prevailing paradigm. When paradigms shift, innovation opens entirely new conceptual territories and generates new wealth." Having someone from the outside can be the difference between looking and seeing.

In the review it is important to collect data onsite through a series of interviews with your management team, as well as with various supervisors and customer service agents in your center. Call flow and workflow processes should be reviewed, actual calls monitored, and supervisors and customer service agents observed during both peak and downtimes. During this analysis, you will uncover your specific operational goals and corporate objectives, and develop a customized strategy to meet those objectives.

Alignment and Processes

Performance management looks at the whole organization to align performance with objectives. By deriving objectives from the overall strategy, it ensures that all people, initiatives and improvements are working towards the organization's goals. This can be accomplished by having an extensive knowledge of the processes that the organization performs to get work done.

Processes define how your organization operates. They are sequences of linked activities that describe the way information and materials are processed. They involve functions, people and equipment, but are not themselves functions—processes can cross functions, and must be understood as a whole.

When processes are defined, there must be owners who will take responsibility for their ongoing improvement. Both internal and external customers must be identified. And everyone must agree with the list of deliverables.

Performance Indicators

The impact of learning on customer service agent performance cannot be underestimated. By improving performance you can minimize variability. This might mean that part of what the performance indicators track are things like the customer service agent's

- transaction preparation,
- transaction execution, and
- transaction follow-up.

You will want to look at various indicators or metrics including those various parts of the process they use to serve customers with

- efficient metrics,
- effective metrics, and
- effective efficiency (Anton and Gustin, 2000).

Identifying learning priorities and strategic skills required for excellence performance indicators measure an organization's progress towards its objectives. They provide a concrete method of quantifying progress towards the organization's goals and an early warning of potential problems. Indicators fulfill four functions:

- They check that the organization is moving towards or meeting its objectives. They measure a spread of financial and non-financial indicators. This helps the organization to take early action to avoid future problems. For example, the number of reported defects and customer returns might give an indirect indication of how customers feel about the organization and so predict future sales.

- They re-enforce whether the organization's assumptions about its strategy and objectives are correct or not. If improvement initiatives fail to have the required effect, this could indicate a problem with the organization's strategy/objectives rather than the failure of the initiative.

- They ensure that the organization supplies the goods and services that are required by the marketplace.

- They also check that the organization complies with the standards and regulations that apply to those markets.

While it is not required to have indicators that measure objectives directly (for example, customer attitude can be measured by several indirect indicators, such as the number of returns and customer complaints), objectives must have indicators. Without them, a company can't tell whether the objectives are being achieved. Once your overriding business objectives have been identified, you will want to create a customized performance strategy to help you meet these goals. Through a structured learning schedule, targeted courseware, and a focus on the overall user experience, the maximum benefits can be achieved.

A performance strategy is a contact-centric iterative process that

- identifies measurable performance indicators that impact the profitability of the customer service center, and

- provides the appropriate instructional methodology, techniques and resources to markedly and measurably improve the performance indicators.

Developing a useful set of performance indicators is not simple. Your team may need to gather a considerable amount of data before deciding which indicators work for the organization. Here are a number of considerations to take into account when designing the indicators (Gilbert, 1978) (Hacker, 2002):

You get what you measure. Measures send people messages about what matters and how they should behave. When the measures are consistent with the organization's strategies, they encourage behaviors that are consistent with that strategy. The right measures enable you to track how well your strategy is being implemented and give you a way of communicating this strategy and encouraging its implementation.

Indicator targets should not be based solely on past performance. Improving sales by 10% each year is good when the competition is improving by only 5% each year. However, it is not a good target when the competition is improving by 40% each year. While this type of benchmarking is useful, targets should not be based only on what other organizations are doing. If Japanese companies had set out to emulate European motorcycle manufacturers, they would not have been able to take over the market. The trick is to identify where the organization wants to be in its market space.

Indicators should be chosen with care. Choosing the wrong indicators can have unintended effects. Most people have heard the story about how customer service center operators, given a target call time of five minutes, made sure that they stayed within target by putting the telephone down after the five minutes were up, whether the call was finished or not.

108

Indicators should be consistent. Indicators should be consistent across different functions and levels. If different departments have inconsistent objectives, optimization of performance in one area may have adverse effects on the organization as a whole because of the problems it causes for other areas. For example, halving the time to produce an important part may have no effect unless similar savings are achieved for other parts and assembly. In fact, overproduction in only one part of the process may cause storage problems.

Indicators should be related. All indicators should ultimately be aimed at measuring progress towards the organization's objectives. It only makes sense to use the level of agent training as an indicator if better training leads to fewer defects, which leads to higher customer satisfaction, which leads to better sales, which ultimately leads to increased profits.

Indicators should be predictive. Because indicators are a tool for steering the organization, it is important to have indicators that give an early warning of future problems. A decrease in the number of sales leads, for example, will probably have an effect on future sales volumes. Therefore, the best performance management systems include leading indicators that enable the organization to take timely action to address potential problems.

Analysis enables you to proactively manage your business, giving you the ability to quickly identify deficiencies before they adversely affect customer service and provide customer service agents with the feedback they need in order to be motivated to improve. With the right performance systems, with the right modules, you can identify problems and performance opportunities in real time (figure 7.5). At any given time, you should be able to see which customer service agents have taken a specific learning module, which have retained the material, and which need extra attention to deliver on your promise of exceptional customer service (figure 7.6).

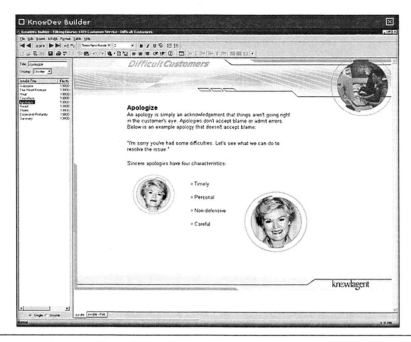

Figure 7.5. Handling difficult customers

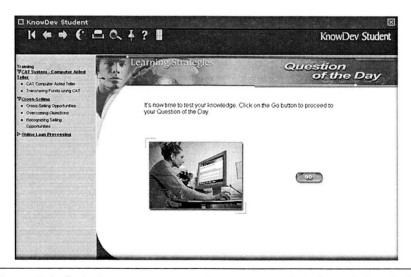

Figure 7.6. Quizzing customer service agent on their knowledge daily is important

Analysis pinpoints individual deficiencies or progress so that you can apply the appropriate coaching. Exercises, reviews and simulations are immediately scored and available before and after training sessions, and you can quickly access a customer service agent's overall performance. Once knowledge gaps have been identified, you should be able to track them down to a single metric. You should also be able to have instant access to your customer service agents' scores. You may want to set up "alerts" to notify you of alarming center-wide trends. These alerts, which can be delivered as an e-mail notification, are a passive, yet proactive management tool that notifies you as soon as a customer service agent falls below defined criteria so that you can automatically assign training (figure 7.7).

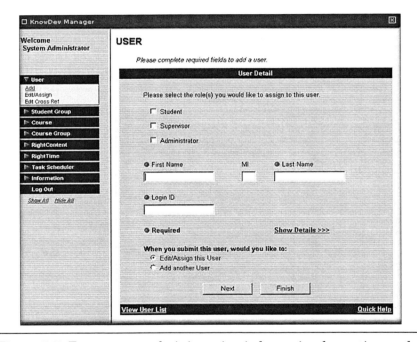

Figure 7.7. Easy system administration is key to implementing real-time training

Monitoring

Monitoring is an essential part of a performance management system. It allows you to

- check that your objectives are being met,
- check the effect of your initiatives,
- highlight problems to be corrected immediately,
- look at performance indicators that go against the trend, and
- check that indicators are providing useful and reliable feedback.

After the performance management system has been implemented and rolled out in your centers, you will want to monitor and measure your progress against the objectives that were identified (figure 7.8). Once these initial goals have been achieved, then you can "turn the dial" to address your center's next set of business objectives.

People at different levels within an organization need different information. A CEO needs to have a high-level, strategic view of how the organization is performing, whereas the sales director needs to have more specific details on the sales, such as the number of sales leads, the number of new customers and so on (Blasidell, 2001). You can monitor indicators using a variety of methods tailored to the specific needs of the people responsible for each area: tables display the raw performance data. They provide a level of detail that cannot be shown in a graphical format. Charts display performance data over a period of time and help identify trends in performance. Dashboards display a snapshot of your performance indicators and provide an overall picture of the current state of the organization.

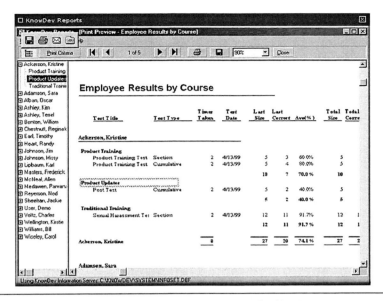

Figure 7.8. Measuring agent performance and effectiveness

A quick and powerful way of checking on the performance of your organization is to use a traffic light system that shows if performance indicators are below target, on target or above target.

Learning Strategy	INTERACTIVE PLANNING	
	Individual Agents	**Supervisors/Mgrs.**
Discovery	• Identify individual knowledge and skill gaps within an agent population	
Opportunity	• Align employee performance with company objectives • Drive employee effectiveness	
Technique	• Simulation, coaching, interactive gaming, recurrent and frequent training delivery	
Timing	• *The most teachable moment* • Deliver training during downtimes in call volume	
Validation	• Results • Success? Failure? To what extent?	

Figure 7.9. Improvement initiatives should meet your organization's objectives

113

Improvement

Improvement initiatives are projects that are specifically designed to meet your organization's objectives. Initiatives should be consistent with the strategy and objectives of your organization (figure 7.9). An initiative aimed at improving the control and monitoring of customer orders has little point unless the initiative can be shown to have positive effects on such things as sales and financial returns. Not only do you have to implement an initiative, you also have to understand how the initiative will contribute to an objective, and be able to quantify its effects. This is used to judge the success of the initiative and to be able to estimate its overall value.

Before implementing a program of initiatives, you must understand the relationships between the indicators in your performance management system. If you decide that improved staff satisfaction will positively affect customer perception, you must be able to predict how those improvements will be translated into increased sales and profitability (Croft, 2002) (Ehbar, 1998). You should also understand how the initiative fits in with other ongoing performance work. While it can be a good idea to improve service to small customers, it is probably more worthwhile to concentrate improvement efforts on more lucrative sectors if those customers contribute only 5% of the organization's revenue.

Performance improvements come from increasing the efficiency and effectiveness of the processes with which your organization delivers goods and services. However, not all processes are equally important. A major step in setting up a process improvement program is to recognize which processes are central to the organization's performance and to concentrate efforts on improving the processes that contribute most towards your goals and objectives.

It is not just one customer service agent's behavior that is important. It is every agent, every day. This means that we need to provide very individualized learning. If we give the customer service agent the attention they personally need, there can be profound impacts on their individual performance.

One place to start is to identify the behaviors required to achieve proficiency across the customer service agent's five to fifteen discrete processes. You will want to teach them to serve your customers and profitably. To them, when they first start, it can feel like drinking from a fire hose. To prevent overwhelming the customer service agents, and quick burn out you will want to consider taking a page from manufacturing. Focus on quality with a goal of execution proficiency, not product knowledge. Retrieving and delivering product/policy/promotion information is simply one of the five to fifteen discrete processes a customer service agent might be expected to do.

It is also important to recognize that the activities in a process are carried out in a logical sequence, not in isolation. This means that, to get the best out of an improvement program, your activities must be designed to work as parts of the whole process, rather than just fitting in with the departments that carry them out.

Mapping processes can help you:

- spot inefficiencies, duplications and bottlenecks where improvements can be made

- decide whether the complexity is necessary

- check if the work is carried out efficiently

- determine if simplifications are possible

- understand if the process is effective

- target improvement initiatives

Once you have made the improvements, you can then return to the strategy and start again (figure 7.1).

Hire Right

Performance management starts by getting the right people in the door in the first place. The customer service "gene" is carried by people who are born to serve. For others, the ability to sell is also a unique "gene." Those two types of skill sets are very important, but very different. In hiring, you will want to look at behavioral interviewing techniques to help you determine if the candidate will fit the position. Some candidates just want a job, without truly understanding what they are great at. Turnover for those put in the wrong position costs the company big time. It is estimated the cost to replace one customer service agent is between $6,000 and $8,000. Employee loyalty? If time to proficiency averages six months, employee commitment is important.

The Behavioral Interviewing Process and Questions

The purpose of behavioral event interviewing (BEI) is to make sure the candidates fit the job characteristics and can meet the business objectives. When behavioral interviewing is employed, employers can expect increased employee productivity and the employee will have increased job satisfaction because the person is well suited for the position (Petouhoff, 2003).

Job competencies are based on drivers and motivators. These include motives, traits, self-image, values, skills and knowledge. To determine if the person will be a valuable asset to the group, in the interviewing process it is important to look for observable behavior that exhibits the competencies required for the job. This model of behavioral interviewing is based on research that has analyzed what top performing people do more often and more effectively for better business results. It also helps to establish in the interviewing process the expectations of the employer with the candidate so that the candidate can better assess whether they are truly interested in the job. The purpose is to have the candidate paint a clear picture for you of what their capabilities and competencies are so that you are not surprised and you feel certain this person can do the job.

You will want to create questions prior to the interview that can elicit detailed information about a candidate's past performance from a behavioral perspective. The reason for this is that past experience is the best indicator of one's ability to apply their competencies to the job you are looking to fill.

Ever see a commercial for the US Army? Unfortunately, those employees can't quit when the reality of boot camp sets in, but your employees can. Realistic job previews during the hiring process can screen out candidates who are going to quit when they get to your "boot camp."

The BEI Process

The BEI process is based on a simple but powerful premise: past behavior is the best predictor of future behavior. The objectives in the BEI process are:

- focus on the details of past performance
- describe the content of the current opening
- make the best candidate choice based on reliable information from the interview

Benefits of the BEI Process

For interviewer, the benefits are:

- provides objective criteria for assessing candidates
- allows the collection of specific details about the candidates work experience
- forces the candidate to provide more than canned responses
- focuses the interview process
- makes the process more uniform from candidate to candidate

For candidate, the benefits are:

- provides a chance to talk about, in detail, their important work experiences
- offers opportunity to highlight strengths, passions and areas of success
- provides the opportunity to reveal their work style, drivers and priorities

Because the candidate goes into more detail, this process can take longer than a normal interview. Many times if there are other people interviewing the candidate, each interview might take a different aspect/competency about the position and probe for the details using the BEI process. Also, the questions you ask are not as important as how you probe the response, since many competencies will be revealed as the candidate speaks regardless of the specific question.

Steps in the BEI

1. State the objective

State that you wish to get a snapshot of what the person looks like in action.

2. Describe the information sought

To get this snapshot, ask the person to describe a work-related event that occurred within the last 18 months. Mention that you wish to probe this event in detail.

3. **Solicit the appropriate event using a behavioral-based question**

   Ask a BEI question designed to elicit evidence of a competency required for the job.

4. **Obtain an overview of the event**

   Before they launch into the story, ask for a "30 second overview" of the event including how it turned out.

5. **Track the entire event in sequence**

   Ask the candidate to recount the event in detail. Track the sequence from the beginning to the end of the story (or whatever point you are interested in starting the story) to its conclusion.

Tracking the Event in the Interview

To begin, say something like...

That was a good overview. Now tell me some of the details. How did the project start?

To get to the next step, say something like...

What were the most important steps after that?

Then what happened next?

What was the key point of your involvement?

When tracking an event, try to get a complete story of an event first.

How did it start?

What were the key points in the event, in sequence?

What were the results?

Ask the candidate:

What did they do, say, think, feel...

Ask what other people did and said:

What did your manager, employees, teammates do, say, think, feel...

Separate the candidate's role from others:

What specifically was your role?

Who is the "we" here?

To get the interview back on track, say something like…

Can you give me more details about that activity?

If I were there, what would I see?

Let's backtrack. When you did that, what was going on?

You said there were meetings involved. Is there one that stands out in your mind?

When Probing An Event

1. After asking the person to think of an event, using the appropriate initial question, obtain a brief overview.

2. Decide if it is a simple, short-duration or a complex, long-duration event.

    a. If it is a short-duration one, immediately ask how the person first got involved and then start tracking the sequence of the person's involvement. Ask for details of the involvement when appropriate and *what happened next?* to move the sequence along.

    b. If it is a complex event:

        i. Ask what were the key points of the person's involvement. Take notes so that you can come back to each point.

        ii. Ask how the person first got involved.

        iii. Ask about the first key point of involvement the person mentioned earlier.

        iv. Ask about the next key point of involvement, etc.

3. When the person describes his/her activity in general terms, ask what the person specifically did and how they did it. For example:

> Interviewee: I made sure they knew what I wanted.
>
> Probe: How did you do that?
>
> Interviewee: I orchestrated the event.
>
> Probe: What specifically did you do?

4. When a person mentions a meeting or a conversation that seems significant, ask for the interviewee's thoughts immediately before it; then ask what the interviewee said and thought during the conversation. Try to get an actual dialogue, for example:

> *Do you remember what you said to her?*

5. Probe the "we."

> *What was your part in the development of the sale?*

6. Probe to get the candidate's thoughts, when he/she mentions doing something that suggests important mental activity, such as making a decision, developing a sales plan, contacting clients, working with alliance partners, fielding objections, closing the sale, maintaining the account...

   a. *How did you come up with your sales plan?*

   b. *How did you handle sales objections? Give me two examples of how you handled them.*

7. Keep the person moving through the sequence of the story by asking, *"What happened next?"* or for complex events, *"What was the key step in terms of your involvement?"* or *"You mentioned that another key part of your involvement was creating a list of potential customers. Tell me specifically how you came up with this list and how you went about contacting them."*

8. When a candidate mentions several similar activities (a series of meetings, talking to several customers, preparing a sales presentation) ask them about one of those activities.

    Tell me more about one of those sales calls that stands out in your mind—either because the call was particularly important or because describing it will give me a sense of what most of the calls were like.

9. If the person describes what they usually do, ask what they actually did in this particular case.

10. At the end of the story, thank the person for the details they provided.

Try not to:

- ask leading questions, i.e., those that telegraph the answer you want such as:
  - o You like to work alone, don't you?
  - o What kind of planning did you do for that meeting?
- accept generalizations,
- let the candidate digress from the event,
- assess the candidate before you hear all of the story,
- summarize or paraphrase what the candidate says, or
- make assumptions about the event that are not supported by the candidate's story.

> ## BEI Tips
>
> - Avoid using the word "why."
> - Using "why" may put the candidate on the defensive and is likely to elicit "socially desirable" responses versus what they did (behavior).
> - Acknowledge when the candidate has given you the information you need.
> - Do not let them go on and on.
> - Get the candidate to stick to the situation you are exploring at the time to get the whole picture.
> - Let the candidate talk as long as he or she stays with the incident.
> - Fill in any gaps in the story by interrupting the candidate's account to ask for details.
> - Take brief notes about each incident and about any points you want to return to later.
> - Use clarifying questions to re-focus the interview if it gets off track.
>
> *—How to Hire the Right Person for the Right Job*, Petouhoff, 2003.

Scripts To Help You Probe

If the interviewee does not say enough about their involvement:

It sounds like you were involved in this project over a long period of time. Since we won't be able to cover everything you did in detail, it would help me if you could first tell me briefly what you believe were the key parts of your involvement. Then we can focus on a couple of them.

Getting them to describe who is "we":

The two of you were involved in this together, but I am especially interested in your involvement. What was your part in the _____?

If the interviewee uses general terms:

Tell me specifically what you were doing in terms of cold calling. Or you had mentioned cold calling. If I had been following you around on the job that week, what would I have seen you do or heard you say?

If the interviewee digresses:

I wish we could spend more time on that, but I need to focus on your involvement in the situation you're describing. Can we go back to point when...?

If the interviewee makes large leaps in a story:

I lost the sequence. Let's go back to the point when_____. What happened after that?

If the interviewee story started years ago, but the significant action occurred in the past year:

Given that we are primarily interested in things you have been involved in within the past year or so, let's start there.

If the interviewee mentions a conversation that appears significant:

I am interested in hearing about that conversation in detail. Where did it take place? Who was there? As you went into the room, what were you thinking? What was the response after you presented the product? What were you thinking then? How did you handle their objections? Can you remember anything else you said?

If the interviewee mentions something that suggests significant mental activity, i.e., planning, organizing, strategizing, closing:

What was going through your mind at that point? What were you thinking? What was your thought process?

If the interviewee interprets someone's attitude or feelings, i.e., "I could tell she was concerned about the reliability of our product."

How could you tell?

If you sense that the interviewee has not described all the details:

Is there anything else you would like to add about your involvement in this situation?

123

If you want to wrap up the story and move on to the next event:

How did this sale turn out?

Thanking the interviewee:

Thank you for telling me about that sales call. I really appreciate how you were able to remember the details of what you thought and said.

Performance Management Certification

Once you have developed your performance management system and process, gathered all your indicators and created a system to measure them, you will want to set up a certification process for customer service agent proficiency. This helps agents when they go through the employee appraisal and development process. If the agents are clear on what proficiencies are required for raises, bonuses and promotions, they will be more likely to hit those targets. During your new hire training you will want to clearly identify and track deficiencies in customer service agent proficiency especially upon exiting initial training. Having these deficiencies identified will allow you to determine exactly what modules the customer service agent needs to become proficient in.

Build Quality In

So what have we learned so far? The goal is to align customer service agent behavior with the objectives of the company. That can be best accomplished by individualized learning to every agent, every day. This process is part of a 4-part process we learned in Chapter 5.

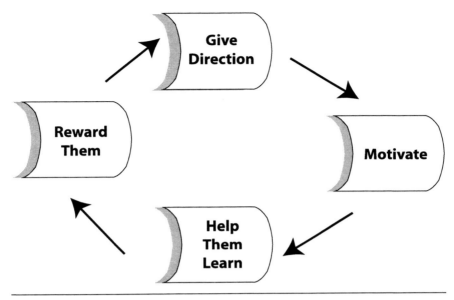

Figure 7.10. The direction, motivation, learning and rewarding cycle in performance management

By providing the right content, at the right time to the right customer service agent you will increase your revenue and sales, and therefore your profit growth.

The four part process entails:

Direction—"Tell me what to do."

Here you will want to give clear and consistent communication of the business objectives (example—we must decrease unnecessary truck rolls).

Motivation—"Tell me why I need to do it."

In this part of the process you will want to provide context for those objectives (example, rolling a repair truck is more expensive than increased handle time to diagnose and fix a problem).

Learning—"Show me how to do it," "Let me practice," "Let me do it."

The profound part of this part is the power of simulation. People learn best by doing and learning the cause and effect relationship.

Reward—"Tell me how I did," "Pay me or penalize me."

Compensation with real time feedback drives agent behavior and performance. People respond to rewards. Because of this natural tendency in all of us, you will want to develop a scorecard. The scorecard can be used to keep track of the customer service agent's performance.

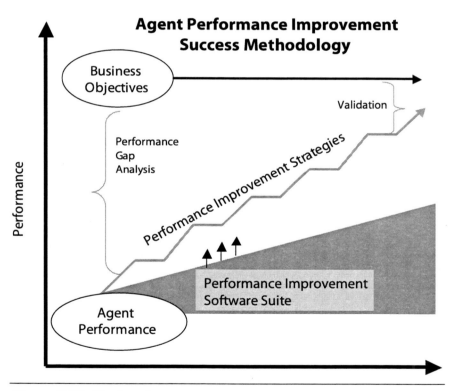

Figure 7.11. Closing the gap

By providing a performance management system that can change customer service agent's behaviors and therefore performance, a company can close the gap between their employee performance and business objectives (figure 7.11). Since salaries are one of the highest costs in operating a business, our research indicates that there is no other choice but to focus the customer service center's resources in this area.

ACD: Automatic Call Distributor. A device that forwards incoming calls to the next available TSR or answering position.

After Tax Net Income (Earnings): Net income before taxes minus income taxes.

Client: A company or organization that uses the services of a customer service center or customer service provider (CSP).

CRM: Customer Relationship Management. A comprehensive suite of sales, marketing and service solutions to provide organizations a full view of customers data in order to serve them better.

CSR: Customer Service Representative. A general term for someone who handles telephone calls in a customer service center. Other common names for the same job include, but are not limited to: CSR, operator, attendant, representative, telephone service representative (TSR).

Earnings per share: After tax net income (earnings) divided by the total number of shares outstanding.

Economic Value Added (EVA): Increased revenue + cost savings.

Gross Margin: Revenue minus the cost of goods and services sold (also known as gross profit).

Internal Rate of Return (IRR): The rate of return that would make the present value of future cash flows plus the final market value of an investment or business opportunity equal to the original investment.

Net Income (Earnings) Before Taxes: Net operating income minus interest and other non-operating expenses.

Net Operating Income (NOI): Income before deducting non-operating expenses such as interest and income taxes. To calculate net operating income, subtract operating expenses (sales and marketing expenses + research and development expenses + administrative expenses + other operating expenses) from gross margin.

Net Present Value (NPV): The present value of an investment's future net cash flows minus the initial investment. Net present value is very meaningful to financial executives, who use it to compare different investment opportunities.

Present Value: The current value of one or more future cash payments, discounted at some appropriate interest rate.

Program: Refers to the services that a customer services provider performs for a client.

Revenue: The total dollar amount collected for goods and services provided.

Adams, J. 1977. Motor Learning and Retention. In *Fundamentals and Applications of Learning*, eds. Marx, M. and Bunch, M. New York: Macmillan.

Adria, Marco, and Shamsud D. Chowdhury. 2002 The Call Center: Changing Skills in the New Workplace. *Tech Republic.com*, 26 February.

Aguayo, Rafael, and W. Edwards Deming. 1991. *Dr. Deming: The American Who Taught the Japanese About Quality*. San Francisco: Fireside.

Allen, Rex J. 1994. Who Had Better Be On First: Getting Optimal Results From Multimedia Training. Chap. 13 in *The McGraw-Hill Multimedia Handbook*. New York: McGraw-Hill, Inc.

Anderson, Cushing. 2000. *e-learning in Practice: Blended Solutions in Action*. IDC White Paper.

ASTD/The Masie Center. 2001. *E-Learning: "If We Built It, Will They Come?"* White Paper.

Atkinson, Hawley, John Hamburg and Christopher Ittner. 1994. *Linking Quality to Profits, Quality-Based Cost Management*. New York: American Society for Quality.

Anton, Jon. 1997. *Call Center Management By the Numbers*. West Lafayette, Indiana: Ichor Business Books, Purdue University Press.

Anton, Jon. 1999. *Call Center Performance Enhancement: Using Simulation and Modeling*. West Lafayette, Indiana: Ichor Business Books, Purdue University Press.

Anton, Jon. 1996. *Customer Relationship Management: Making Hard Decisions with Soft Numbers*. Upper Saddle River, New Jersey: Prentice-Hall.

Anton, Jon. 1997. *Listening to the Voice of the Customer*. New York: The Customer Service Group.

Anton, Jon. 1994. Internal research report. West Lafayette, Indiana: Purdue University Center for Custom-Driven Quality.

Anton, Jon., R. Bennett, and R. Widdows. 1994. *Call-Center Design and Implementation*. Houston: Dame Publications.

Anton, Jon., and David Gustin. 2000. *Call Center Benchmarking: How Good Is Good Enough?"* West Lafayette, Indiana: Ichor Business Books, Purdue University Press.

Anton, Jon., and J.C. de Ruyter. 1991. Van Klachten naar Managementinformatie. *Harvard Holland Review* 27 (Fall).

Anton, Jon. and Natalie L. Petouhoff. 2002. *CRM: The Bottom-line To Optimizing Your ROI.* Upper Saddle River, New Jersey: Prentice Hall.

Anton, Jon., Natalie L. Petouhoff and Lisa M. Schwartz. 2002. *Integrating People with Processes and CRM Technology*. Santa Maria, CA: The Anton Press.

Anton, Jon., and Bob Vilsoet. 2003. *Customer Relationship Management Technology: Infrastructure for Customer Collaboration*. Santa Maria, CA: The Anton Press.

Anton, Jon, and Laurent Philonenko. 2001. *20:20 CRM A Visionary Insight Into Unique Customer Contact*. Santa Maria, CA: The Anton Press.

Anton, Jon, Anita Rockwell and Teresa Setting. 2003. *The Impact of Call Centers on Company Image*. White Paper. Santa Maria, CA: The Anton Press.

Barker, Joel. 1993. *Paradigms: The Business of Discovering the Future*. New York: Harper and Row.

Blasidell, Mikael. 2001. Breaking Out of The Box: Using Customer Data, *Customer Support Management*, January. p. 28.

Bluvband, Zigmund. 2002. *Quality's Greatest Hits: Classic Wisdom From the Leaders of Quality*. Washington, D.C.: American Society for Quality.

Bridging The Gap Between Executive Vision and Agent Performance. 2002 Knowlagent White Paper. <www.knowlagent.com>.

Brockbank , Bray J. May the E-Learning Workforce Be With You, .2001 Part of the *NewsFactor Network*,. 27 July. <www.osOpinion.com>

Clark, Donald. 2002. <www.nwlink.com/~donclark/hrd/history/history.html>.

Conner, Marcia. 2000. *Adult Learning*. <www.Learnativity.com>

Consortium for Advanced Manufacturing International (CAM-I). 2001. The Road to Excellence. *The CAM-I Process Management Guide*.

Craig, Robert L. 1996. *The ASTD Training & Development Handbook*. New York: McGraw-Hill.

Croft, Kimberly. 2002. Where Your Profits Went: Employee Turnover.*Contact Professional*. January/February, p. 29.

Cross, Patricia. 1992. *Adults as Learners: Increasing Participation and Facilitating Learning*. New York: Jossey-Bass.

Delphi Group. 2000. *Need to Know: Integrating e-learning with High Velocity Value Chain.*, White Paper.

Deming, W. E. 1986. *Out of Crisis*. Cambridge, MA: MIT.

Deming, W. E. 2000. *The New Economics for Industry, Government, Education*. 2nd Edition. Boston: MIT Press.

Drucker, P. F. 1979. *Adventures of a Bystander*. New York: Harper & Row.

Dull, Stephen, Timothy Stephens and Mark Wolfe. 2002. How Much Are Customer Relationships Really Worth? *Accenture Study*. <www.accenture.com/xd/xd.asp?it=enweb&xd=industries%5Ccommunications%5Ccommunications%5Ccomm_crmstudy.xml/>

Ehrbar, Al. 1998. *Economic Value Added: The Real Key To Creating Wealth*. New York: Wiley and Sons, Inc.

Fitz-Eng, Jac. 1994. Yes...You Can Weigh Training's Value. *Training Magazine,* July.

Fleischer, Joe. 2001. A Mecca for Customers' calls: Call Routing, *Call Center Magazine*. June, p. 67.

Fleischer, Joe. 2001. A Sharper Image on Quality: 5 Call Centers Improve Agent Communication via Monitoring, Training and Customer Feedback. *Call Center Magazine*. July. p. 90.

Forman, David C. 1994. An ROI Model for Multimedia Programs. *Multimedia Today*. Volume 2, Issue 3.

Gagne, Robert M. (Ed.) 1987. *Instructional Technology: Foundations*. New York: Lawrence Erlbaum Association.

Gilbert, Tom. 1978. *Human Competence: Engineering Worthy Performance*. New York: McGraw-Hill.

Goldratt, Eliyahu. 1997. *Critical Chain*. Great Barrington, MA: The North River Press.

Goodman, John and Steve Newman. 2002. Understand Customer Behavior and Complaints. *Quality Progress*, Vol. 35, no. 1

Greengard, Samuel. 2002. The Evolution of Retail: Wireless, Electronic Point-of-sale and e-learning. *IQ Magazine*, March/April.

Guthrie, E. R. 1952. *The Psychology of Learning*. New York: Harper & Row.

Hacker, Stephen, and Marsha Willard. 2001. *The Trust Imperative: Performance Improvement Through Productive Relationships*. Washington, D. C.: American Society for Quality.

Hall, Brandon 1995. Multimedia Training's Return on Investment. *Workforce Training News*, July/August.

Hamel, Gary. 1999. The Search for the Young and Gifted. *BusinessWeek,* 4 October.

Hawkin, Paul. 1993. *The Ecology of Commerce: A Declaration of Sustainability*. New York: HarperBusiness.

Hergenhahn, B. R. and M.A. Olson. 1982. *An Introduction to Theories of Learning*. 2nd edition. Englewood Cliffs, New Jersey: Prentice-Hall, Inc.

Hersch, Warren, Lee Hollman and Jennifer O'Herron. 2001. Think of Your Employees as Your Best Customers. *Call Center Magazine*. December. p. 30.

Heskett, J., W. E. Sasser, and L. Schlesinger. 1997. *The Service Profit Chain*. New York: The Free Press.

Hickman, E. Stewart. 2000. Pay the Person, Not the Job. *Training & Development*. October. p. 52.

<http://www.coe.uh.edu/courses/cuin6373/idhistory/index.html>

<http://www-cscl95.indiana.edu/cscl95/wiburg.html>

Hull, C. L.. 1943. *Principles of Behavior*. Englewood Cliffs, N.J.: Prentice-Hall.

James, Gary, 2001. *Advantages and Disadvantages of Online Learning*. Allen Communications White Paper. <www.allencomm.com>.

Joinson, Carla. 2001. Making Sure Employees Measure Up. *HR Magazine*, March. p. 36.

Juran, J. M., and A. Blanton Godfrey. 1998. *Juran's Quality Handbook*. 5th edition. New York: McGraw-Hill Professional.

Kanigel, Robert. 1997. *The One Best Way: Frederick Winslow Taylor and the Enigma of Efficiency*. New York: Viking Penguin.

Kolb, David. 1983. *Experiential Learning: Experience as the source of learning and development*. New York, Prentice Hall.

Kounadis, Tim, 2001. *E-Learning and Knowledge Management at the Crossroads*. <www.osOpinion.com>, and the NewsFactor Network, 17 July.

Kouzes, James M., and Barry Z. Posner 1995. *The Leadership Challenge*. San Francisco: Jossey-Bass Publishers.

Laabs, Jennifer. 2001. Serving Up a new Level of customer Service via Training at Quebecor: The World's Largest Printing Company. *Workforce*, March, p. 40.

Leeds, Dorothy, 2000. The Power of Questions. *Training & Development,* October, p. 20.

Leigh, Douglas. 1999. *A Brief History of Instructional Design*. <www.pignc-ispi.com/articles/education/brief history.htm>.

Lian, T. 1994. Helping hands. *Bank Marketing* 25 (February).

Liker, Jeffery. 1997. *Becoming Lean: Inside Stories of U.S. Manufacturers*. New York: Productivity Press.

Maslow, A. 1954. *Motivation and Personality*. New York: Harper & Row.

McGarvey, R. 1995. The big thrill. *Entrepreneur* 86 (July).

Microsoft Bookshelf. *Kung Fu-tse in Chinese Philosophy, Socrates in Greek Philosophy*.

Millbank, G. 1994. *Writing Multi-media Training with Integrated Simulation,* paper presented at the Writer's retreat on Interactive Technology and Equipment. Vancouver, Canada.

Morgan, Ronald, and Jack E. Smith. 1996. *Staffing the New Workplace: Selecting and Promoting for Quality Improvement*. New York: American Society for Quality.

Morphy, Erika. 2002. The 21st Century Call Center Rep. *CRMDaily.com*, 28 February.

Nadler, Leonard. 1984. *The Handbook Of Human Resource Development*. (pp. 1.6-1.14 and 6.4-6.12) New York: John Wiley & Sons.

Nelson, Elisabeth. 2001. Users of e-learning Still In Minority. *Tech Republic.com*, 27 November.

Petouhoff, Natalie L. 2003. *How to Hire the Right Person for the Right Job: The Secrets to Behavioral Interviewing*. Upper Saddle River, New Jersey: Prentice Hall.

Petouhoff, Natalie L., and Tanya L. Koons. 2003. *Employee Development: The Key to A Company's Bottom-line Performance*. Upper Saddle River, New Jersey: Prentice Hall.

Rauch, Erwin, and John B. Washbush. 1998. *High Quality Leadership: Practical Guidelines to Becoming a More Effective Manager*. Washington, D. C.: American Society for Quality.

Reckon, Neil. 2001. *Process Management in Marketing and Sales: How To Improve Customer Service*. The Quality Management Forum, vol 27, no 4, Fall, p. 6.

Reichheld, F. F. 1996. *The Loyalty Effect: The Hidden Force Behind Growth, Profits, and Lasting Value*. Boston: Harvard Business School Press.

Reichheld, F. F., and W. E. Sasser Jr. 1990. Zero defects: Quality comes to services. *Harvard Business Review* 106 (September/October).

Robinson, Dana, and James Robinson 1989. *Training for Impact*. San Francisco: Jossey-Bass Publishers.

Roethlein, Christopher, and Paul Mangiameli.2002. Quality In U.S. Manufacturing Industries: An Empirical Study. *American Society for Quality*, vol 9, Issue 3.

Rust, Roland T., Valarie A. Zeithaml, and Katherine N. Lemon. 2002. *Driving Customer Equity: How Customer Lifetime Value is Reshaping Corporate Strategy*, New York: Free Press.

Rust, R. T., A. J. Zahorik, and T. L Keiningham. 1994. *Return on Quality*. Chicago: Probus Publishing Company.

Ruttenbur, Brian, and Ginger Spickler and Sebastian Lurie. 2000. *e-Learning: The Engine of the Knowledge Economy*. Morgan Keegan White Paper, 6 July.

Saettler, L. Paul. 1968. *A History of Instructional Technology*. New York: McGraw-Hill.

Schmitt, Debra, Robert Caruso and Sarah Reines. 2001. Delighting Your Clients: 6 Strategies to Ensure A Quality Customer Experience. *Call Center Professional*, December, p. 32.

Schueler, Judy, 2000. Customer Service Through Leadership. *Training & Development,* October, p. 26.

Shea-Schultz, Heather, and John Fogarty. 2002. *Online Learning Today*. San Francisco: Berrett-Koehler.

Shetty, Y. K. 1993. The quest for quality excellence: Lessons from the Malcolm Baldrige Quality Award. *Advanced Management Journal* 37 (Spring).

Shewhart, Walter A., and W. Edwards Deming. 1986. *Statistical Method from the Viewpoint of Quality Control*. Boston: Dover.

Siebel Journal. 2002. *Customer Satisfaction: The Fundamental Basis of Business Survival*, vol. 5, no.1, pp. 19 and 43.

Sleight, Deborah A. 1993. *A Developmental History of Training. December.* <www.msu.edu/~sleightd/trainhst.html>.

Sliverman, Lori, and Annabeth Propst. 1999. *Critical Shift: The Future of Quality in Organizational Performance.* Washington, D.C.: American Society for Quality.

Star, Karen. 2002. Technology Grows Up. Selling Power. In *Super Sales Manager's Source Book*, vol. 21, no 10, p. 43.

Stamps, David. 1999. So Long 20th Century, *Training Magazine, December, pp. 30-48.*

Slywotzky, Adrian J., and Richard Wise. 2002. The Growth Crisis-- and How to Escape It. *Harvard Business Review*, 1 July.

Taylor, Frederick W. 1911. *The Principles of Scientific Management.* Reprint 1998. New York: Dover.

The Institute for Learning Styles Research. 1999. <www.learningstyles.org>.

Thorndike, Edward. 1928. *Adult Learning.* Boston: AMS Press.

Tough, Allen. 1968. *Why Adults Learn: A Study of the Major Reasons for Beginning and Continuing a Learning Project.* Toronto: Ontario Institute for Studies in Education..

Tough, Allen. 1979. The Adult's Learning Projects. *Research in Education Series No. 1.* Toronto: Ontario Institute for Studies in Education.

Walton, Mary, and W. E. Deming. 1988. *Deming Management Method.* Perige: New York.

Weinsten, Bob. 2001. Customer Needs Drive Contact-Center Job Skills. *Tech Republic.com,* 5 December.

Weiss, Ruth Palombo. 2000. Memory and Learning. *Training & Development,* October, p. 46.

Woods, John A., and Cortada, James W. 1997. *The 1997 ASTD Training and Performance Yearbook,* pp. 3-13. New York: McGraw-Hill.

Yerkes, Robert M., and John D. Dodson. 1908. The Relation of Strength of Stimulus to Rapidity of Habit-Formation. *Journal of Comparative Neurology and Psychology,* 18, pp. 459-482.

Zeithaml, V., A. Parasuraman, L. L. Berry. 1990. *Delivering Quality Service.* New York: The Free Press.

8

85/15 rule, 44

A

Accenture, 3, 4, 5, 7, 96, 133
activist learning style, 79
Adams, J., 65
adult learning theory, 64
Allen, Charles, 70
American Customer
 Satisfaction Index (ACSI),
 8
apprenticeship, 66, 68, 81
AT&T, 6, 7, 96, 100
AT&T Broadband, 100
automatic call distributor
 (ACD), 88, 92

B

Barker, Joel, 106
behavioral event interviewing
 (BEI), 116–24

C

call simulations, 93, 94, 95
Center for Customer-Driven
 Quality, Purdue University,
 15, 55
chinese philosophers, 64
CitiFinancial, 100
computer telephony
 integration (CTI), 92
computer-based training
 (CBT), 84
Conner, Marcia, 81
customer relationship
 management (CRM), 88

customer service agent-to-
 trainer ratio, 78

D

Deming Chain Reaction, 43, 44
Deming, Dr. W. Edwards, 1,
 43–54
Deming's 14 Points, 54
Discovery Learning, 64

E

effectiveness measurements,
 24, 107
efficiency measurements, 24,
 107
enterprise routing, 21–22
Eureka, origins of, 64

F

Ford, 50
Fornell, Claes, 5, 7, 8
Forum Group, 15

G

Gartner, 9, 10
Garza, Theresa, 61
Gilbert, Tom, 108
Greek philosophers, 65, 101

H

Hamel, Gary, 5
Harvard Business Review, 2,
 8, 26, 63
Herbart, Johann Friedrich, 69,
 70
Hull, C. L., 67

I

Institute for Learning Styles
  Research, 82
Ishikawa, 48

J

Juran, Dr. Joseph, 43, 44, 48
JUSE, 49

K

key performance indicators
  (KPIs), 106–9
King, Bob, 49
Knowlagent, 9
Knowles, Malcolm, 64
Kolb, David, 79, 80, 81
Komatsu Tractor, 48

M

MacArthur, General Douglas,
  48
management by results, 45,
  46, 104
manufacturing similarities,
  26, 45, 52
McCarthy, Charles, 49
Millbank, G., 82

P

perceptual learning styles, 82
Piaget, Jean, 64, 65
pragmatist learning style, 80

profit, flywheel, 5–6

Q

Quality Function Deployment
  (QFD), 48

R

reflector learning style, 79
Ritter, Diane, 49
Rust, Roland, 7, 9

S

Smith, Laurence, 49
statistical process control
  (SPC), 47
SWOT analysis, 103

T

theorist learning style, 80
Thorndike, Edward, 63
Total Quality Control (TQC),
  48, 49

V

vestibule training, 68

W

work force management
  (WFM), 88

Y

Yerkes, Robert M., 71

Co-Author

Dr. Jon Anton (also known as "Dr. Jon") is the director of benchmark research at Purdue University's Center for Customer-Driven Quality. He specializes in enhancing customer service strategy through inbound call centers, and e-business centers, using the latest in telecommunications (voice), and computer (digital) technology. He also focuses on using the Internet for external customer access, as well as Intranets and middleware.

Since 1995, Dr. Jon has been the principal investigator of the Purdue University Call Center Benchmark Research. This data is now collected at the BenchmarkPortal.com Web site, where it is placed into a data warehouse that currently contains over ten million data points on call center performance. Based on the analysis of this data, Dr. Jon authors the following monthly publications: "The Purdue Page" in *Call Center Magazine*, "Dr. Jon's Benchmarks" in *Call Center News*, "Dr. Jon's Industry Statistics" in *Customer Interface Magazine*, and "Dr. Jon's Business Intelligence" in the *Call Center Manager's Report*.

Dr. Jon has assisted over 400 companies in improving their customer service strategy/delivery by the design and implementation of inbound and outbound call centers, as well as in the decision-making process of using teleservice providers for maximizing service levels while minimizing costs per call. In August of 1996, *Call Center Magazine* honored Dr. Jon by selecting him as an Original Pioneer of the emerging call center industry. In October of 2000, Dr. Jon was named to the Call Center Hall of Fame. In January of 2001, Dr. Jon was selected for the industry's "Leaders and Legends" Award by Help Desk 2000. Dr. Jon is also a member of the National Committee for Quality Assurance.

Dr. Jon has guided corporate executives in strategically re-positioning their call centers as robust customer access centers through a combination of benchmarking, re-engineering, consolidation, outsourcing, and Web-enablement. The resulting single point of contact for the customer allows business to be conducted anywhere, anytime, and in any form. By better understanding the customer lifetime value, Dr. Jon has developed techniques for calculating the ROI for customer service initiatives.

Dr. Jon has published 96 papers on customer service and call center methods in industry journals. In 1997, one of his papers on self-service was awarded the best article of the year by *Customer Relationship Management Magazine*.

Dr. Jon has published twenty-one professional books:

> *Customer Service and the Human Experience: We, the People, Make the Difference,* The Anton Press, 2003
>
> *Managing Web-Based Customer Experience: Self-service Integrated with Assisted Service*, The Anton Press, 2003
>
> *Customer Service at a Crossroads: What You Do Next to Improve Performance Will Determine Your Company's Destiny*, The Anton Press, 2003
>
> *Offshore Outsourcing Opportunities*, The Anton Press, 2002
>
> *Optimizing Outbound Calling: The Strategic Use of Predictive Dialers*, The Anton Press, 2002
>
> *Customer Relationship Management Technology: Building the Infrastructure for Customer Collaboration*, The Anton Press, 2002
>
> *Customer Obsession: Your Roadmap to Profitable CRM,* The Anton Press, 2002
>
> *Integrating People with Process and Technology*, The Anton Press, 2002
>
> *Selecting a Teleservices Partner*, The Anton Press, 2002
>
> *How to Conduct a Call Center Performance Audit: A to Z,* The Anton Press, 2002
>
> *20:20 CRM A Visionary Insight into Unique Customer Contact*, The Anton Press, 2001
>
> *Minimizing Agent Turnover*, The Anton Press, 2001
>
> *e-Business Customer Service*, The Anton Press, 2001
>
> *Customer Relationship Management, The Bottom Line to Optimizing Your ROI*, Prentice Hall, 2nd Edition, 2001

Call Center Performance Enhancement Using Simulation and Modeling, Purdue University Press, 2000

Call Center Benchmarking: How Good is "Good Enough", Purdue University Press, 1999

Listening to the Voice of the Customer, Alexander Communications, 1997

Contact Center Management by the Numbers, Purdue University Press, 1997

Customer Relationship Management: Making Hard Decisions with Soft Numbers, Prentice-Hall, Inc., 1996

Inbound Customer Contact Center Design, Dame Publishers, Inc., 1994

Computer-Assisted Learning, Hafner Publishing, Inc., 1985

Dr. Jon is the editor for a series of professional books entitled *Customer Access Management*, published by the Purdue University Press.

Dr. Jon's formal education was in technology, including a Doctorate of Science and a Master of Science from Harvard University, a Master of Science from the University of Connecticut, and a Bachelor of Science from the University of Notre Dame. He also completed a three-summer intensive Executive Education program in Business at the Graduate School of Business at Stanford University.

Dr. Jon can be reached at 765.494.8357 or at <DrJonAnton@BenchmarkPortal.com>.

Co-Author

 **Matt McConnell** is the founder and Vice President of Marketing at Knowlagent. In 1995, Matt McConnell founded Knowlagent with his partner John McIwaine with the idea that performance technology needed to be integrated into the workplace to successfully address the knowledge and skill gaps that occur in the service channels of most companies. Through the use of computer networks, McConnell discovered that performance improvement technology delivered directly to the employee desktops could dramatically and immediately impact customer satisfaction, retention and profitability.

For the past seven years, McConnell has dedicated his life's work to re-align the customer service center performance measurement paradigm to reflect the changing landscape of business where service is the differentiator and the customer is King. Because of his vision and technology innovation, McConnell has been recognized as an industry thought leader and has been invited to participate in several annual, high-profile industry events such as a the International Call Center Management conference held in Chicago, the Call Center and CRM Conference in Las Vegas and Call Center Campus in conjunction with Purdue University.

Knowlagent was built from the idea that people are an organization's greatest asset and that without them there would be no relationship or CRM to worry about. McConnell's entrepreneurial spirit has gone against the grain and is pushing corporate America to rethink its view of the customer service agent and the impact these individuals have on corporate goals. Ultimately, relationships happen between people and McConnell's foresight and technology innovation is making sure that the people are prepared.

Industry pundits, press and research analysts have recognized Knowlagent and its founder for his thought leadership and the product's technological superiority. Most recently, Knowlagent was named the market leader for customer service center e-learning in North America by Frost & Sullivan, a leading industry analyst organization. Knowlagent's solution was named "Product of the Year" by *Call Center Magazine* in 1999 and has since won in 2000 and 2002. For a second consecutive year, Knowlagent's was name a winner in *Customer Inter@ction Solutions'* annual "CRM Excellence Awards," and the company was named one of the 50 fastest growing private companies in Atlanta by the Atlanta Business Chronicle in 2002 and again in 2003.

McConnell graduated from the Georgia Institute of Technology with a Bachelor's degree in Industrial and Systems Engineering.

Also available from BenchmarkPortal, Inc.

20:20 CRM A Visionary insight into unique customer contacts
The contact center is at the heart of many businesses today, and CRM initiatives are making customer contact even more critical to the health of every company. 20:20 CRM provides a strategic view of where businesses should be going with their customer contact operation, with practical examples of how to get there.
ISBN 0-9630464-5-4   *By: Dr. Jon Anton and Laurent Philonenko*   **Price: $24.95**

Benchmarking for Profits!
Done right, and done regularly, benchmarking provides improved work life, career advancement and substantially increased earnings on a consistent basis. This book is an essential manual for continuous improvement peer group benchmarking that shows convincingly why proper professionalism in today's environment requires benchmarking. Includes valuable information on how to benchmark through BenchmarkPortal and describes the latest products to help you get the most from this crucial activity.
ISBN 0-9719652-1-8   *By: Bruce Belfiore*   **Price: $11.95**

Call Center Benchmarking "How 'good' is good enough?"
This "how to" book describes the essential steps of benchmarking a call center with other similar call centers, with an emphasis on "self assessment." The reader learns how to plan a benchmark, how to collect the correct performance data, how to analyze the data, and how to find improvement initiatives based on the findings.
ISBN 1-55753-215-X   *By: Dr. Jon Anton*   **Price: $39.95**

Call Center Performance Enhancement - Using Simulation and Modeling
This book provides its readers with an understanding about the role, value, and practical deployment of simulation - an exciting technology for the planning, management, and analysis of call centers. The book provides useful guidelines to call center analysts, managers, and consultants who may be investigating or are considering the use of simulation as a vehicle in their business to responsibly manage change.
ISBN 1-55753-182-X   *By: Jon Anton, Vivek Bapat, Bill Hall*   **Price: $48.95**

Customer Obsession: Your Roadmap to Profitable CRM
Finally, here is a book that covers the complete "journey" of CRM implementation. Ad Nederlof and Dr. Jon Anton have done the near impossible: to position CRM in such a way that it makes practical sense to C-level executives. Beginning with the title of the book, "Customer Obsession," on through the last chapter, this book positions CRM for what it really is, namely, a complete change in corporate strategy, from the top down, that brings the customer into focus.
ISBN 0-9719652-0-X   *By: Ad Nederlof and Dr. Jon Anton*   **Price: $24.95**

Customer Relationship Management: The Bottom Line to Optimizing Your ROI
Customer Relationship Management recommends effective initiatives toward improving customer service and managing change. Creative methodologies are geared toward building relationships through customer-perceived value instruments, monitoring customer relationship indices, and changing the corporate culture and the way people work.
ISBN 0-13-099069-8   *By Dr. Jon Anton and Natalie L. Petouhoff*   **Price: $33.33**

Also available from BenchmarkPortal, Inc.

Customer Relationship Management Technology "Building the Infrastructure for Customer Collaboration"

From our research on the American consumer, it has become very clear that potentially the best customer service strategy is "to offer every possible channel for the customer to help themselves, i.e., self-service." Customer actuated service is mostly driven by technology, and the "art" of self-service is to ensure that the technology is intuitive, easy to use, and that the customer is rewarded for "having done the job themselves." This book delves into all the technology solutions that enable self-service. The reader will find a robust description of the technology alternatives, and many examples of how self-service is saving companies money, while at the same time satisfying customers.

ISBN 0-9630464-7-0 *By Dr. Jon Anton and Bob Vilsoet* **Price: $39.99**

Customer Service and the Human Experience: We, the People, Make the Difference

One of the leading challenges for today's managers is the training and motivating of excellent agents. While much attention has been focused on the technology and benefits of providing multiple channels for customer contact, little attention has been paid to handling the human part of the equation—training CSRs to field more than just telephone communications. Great statistics and benchmarking help the customer service/call center professional keep ahead of the ever-changing business environment as the authors successfully blend the critical human aspect of the center with the ever growing need for metrics and the bottom line.

ISBN 0-9719652-7-7 *By Dr. Rosanne D'Ausilio and Dr. Jon Anton* **Price: $34.95**

Customer Service at a Crossroads: What You Do Next to Improve Performance Will Determine Your Company's Destiny

By consistently delivering information about products, services and information to customer service agents, based on their individual skill levels—at the right time in the right way, organizations are also delivering a consistent, clear understanding of corporate objectives and vision. The result: thousands of customer interactions that delight the customer and improve retention as well as corporate profitability. Optimizing agent performance can quickly deliver incredible returns beyond customer loyalty. That is what this book is all about.

ISBN 0-9719652-6-9 *By Matt McConnell and Dr. Jon Anton* **Price: $15.95**

e-Business Customer Service

With the advent of e-business technology, we suddenly find ourselves with completely different customer service channels. The old paradigms are gone forever. This books details how to measure and manage e-business customer service. The book describes the key performance indicators for these new channels, and it describes how to manage by these new rules of engagement with specific metrics. Managing customer service in this "new age" is different, it is challenging, and it is impossible to migrate from the old to the new without reading this book.

ISBN 0-9630464-9-7 *By Dr. Jon Anton and Michael Hoeck* **Price: $44.00**

How to Conduct a Call Center Performance Audit: A to Z

Call centers are an important company asset, but also a very expensive one. By learning to conduct a performance audit, readers will be able to understand over fifty specific aspects of a call center that must be running smoothly in order to achieve maximum performance in both efficiency and effectiveness of handling inbound customer calls.

ISBN 0-9630464-6-2 *By Dr. Jon Anton and Dru Phelps* **Price: $34.99**

Integrating People with Process and Technology

This book contains valuable information regarding the "people" side of technology initiatives. Many companies buy the best hardware and software, and spend thousands of dollars implementing technology only to find out that the employees resist the changes, and do not fully adopt the new, and possibly, improved processes. By understanding how to manage people during change, managers will see a much quicker ROI on their technology initiatives.

ISBN 0-9630464-3-8 *By Jon Anton, Natalie Petouhoff, & Lisa Schwartz* **Price: $39.99**

Listening to the Voice of the Customer

With the help of this book, the professional skills you need to measure customer satisfaction will lead you to different approaches until you have found the one that best fits you, your company, and your organization's culture.

ISBN 0-915910-43-8 *By Dr. Jon Anton* **Price: $33.95**

6/3/2003

Also available from BenchmarkPortal, Inc.

Managing Web-Based Customer Experiences: Self-Service Integrated with Assisted-service
The time to grow your call center into a multi-channel customer contact center is now. This book has the power to help you increase customer satisfaction through the implementation of Web self-service. The value of this book can be calculated in terms of calls deflected from your call center, increased customer retention, an ultimately in a healthy return on your investment. In this book, the authors take you step-by-step through the best practices that lead to a successful self and assisted-service strategy.
ISBN 0-9719652-4-2 *By Dr. Jon Anton and Mike Murphy* **Price: $35.95**

Minimizing Agent Turnover
Some agent turnover can be functional, but most turnover is dysfunctional and can be very expensive. This book explores the types of turnover, including internal versus external; and documents the typical causes of agent turnover. Most importantly, this book describes a methodology for diagnosing the root causes of your agent turnover, and suggests improvement initiatives to minimize agent turnover at your customer contact center.
ISBN 0-9630464-2-X *By Dr. Jon Anton and Anita Rockwell* **Price: $39.99**

Offshore Outsourcing Opportunities
For call center executives wanting to explore and understand the benefits of offshore outsourcing, the authors have brought together 'under one cover' a comprehensive guide that takes the reader through each step of the complex issues of outsourcing customer service telephone calls to agents in another country. With the pressure of today's competitive climate forcing companies to take a hard look at providing higher quality customer services at lower costs, this book is a "must read" for every call center executive.
ISBN 0-9719652-3-4 *By Dr. Jon Anton and John Chatterley* **Price: $34.99**

Optimizing Outbound Calling: The Strategic Use of Predictive Dialers
The content of the book is organized in such a way as to assist the reader in understanding the complete end-to-end process of automated outbound call dialing. Specifically, the reader will find the following steps described in detail: a) preparing a needs assessment, b) selecting and contracting a predictive dialer supplier, c) implementing a predictive dialer solution, d) applying change management principles to ensure "buy-in" by existing agents, d) handling and using dialer reports, and finally, e) benchmarking dialer improvements to ensure attaining the anticipated ROI.
ISBN 0-9719652-2-6 *By Jon Anton and Alex G. Demczak* **Price: $39.99**

Selecting a Teleservices Partner
This book tackles one of today's hottest topics: Customer Contact Outsourcing. Companies are in a quandary about the myriad of teleservices questions they're faced with, such as deciding to outsource, cost / benefit analysis, RFP development, proposal assessment, vendor selection, contractual requirements, service level performance measurement, and managing an ongoing teleservices relationship. With the authors help, readers will find this complex issue straightforward to approach, understand, and implement.
ISBN 0-9630464-8-9 *By Jon Anton and Lori Carr* **Price: $34.99**

The Four-Minute Customer
This is a very unique book directed at developing and maintaining "Top Reps" that are uniquely motivated to deliver the highest possible quality of caller customer service at your center. Learn what it takes to find and lead the best of the best. Don't settle for mediocrity. Instead, learn how to manage the best in class customer contact center by attracting and keeping Top Reps at your organization.
ISBN 0-9630464-1-1 *By Michael Tamer* **Price: $34.99**

Wake Up Your Call Center: Humanizing Your Interaction Hub, 3ʳᵈ edition
With new and up-to-date material, this third edition speaks volumes about the need to reinforce the human element in the equation. This is a straight forward guide for humanizing the impersonal, with practical to-do's, real life examples, and applications to delight your customers. In depth chapters include mixed messages, change and stress management, conflict resolution, rapport building, and communicating powerfully, just to mention a few.
ISBN 1-55753-217-6 *By Rosanne D'Ausilio, Ph.D* Price: $44.95

Order Form

Secure online ordering is available at: www.benchmarkportal.com/bookstore

Billing Information: **Shipping Information** (if different):

| Name |
| Company |
| Address |
| Address 2 |
| City/St/Zip |
| Phone |

Please charge my: ____ **American Express**   ____ **Discover**

                        ____ **Mastercard**   ____ **Visa**

Card Number

Expiration Date

Signature

I've enclosed a check in the amount of

Purchase Order Number

Book Title	Amt*	Qty	Total
		Books Total	
		Shipping and Handling	
For all U.S. addresses, $5.00 for the first book, $3.00 for each additional book.			
*For all International addresses, books must be **pre-paid** and must include a shipping and handling charge of $25.00 for the first book and $10 for each additional book.*			
		Total Amount Due**	

*Call for volume and pre-order discounts available (805-614-0123 Ext. 10)

**State sales tax will be added where applicable

For other books, tapes, and videos visit our online store:

http://www.benchmarkportal.com/bookstore

Send all orders to:

BenchmarkPortal, Inc.

3130 Skyway Drive, Suite 702

Santa Maria, CA 93455-1817

For quick service, fax your order to: (805) 614-0055

For questions about your order, please call: (805) 614-0123 Ext. 10

6/3/2003

Industry Reports Available From BenchmarkPortal, Inc.

Secure online ordering is available at:
http://www.benchmarkportal.com/bookstore

or call (805) 614-0123 Ext. 20

These industry reports contain hundreds of call center benchmarks and best practices for a specific industry:

Aerospace

Airline

All Industries

Automotive

Banking

Brokerage

Cable Television

Catalog

Computer Hardware

Computer Products

Computer Software

Credit Card

Financial Services

Government & Non-Profit

Healthcare Provider

Help Desk

Insurance

Insurance – Health

Insurance – Life

Insurance – Property & Casualty

Outbound Teleservices

Publishing & Media

Retail

Technical Support

Telecommunications

Transportation

Travel & Hospitality

Utilities

Wireless